Four Corners

Jack C. Richards · David Bohlke
with Kathryn O'Dell

3

Workbook

CAMBRIDGE
UNIVERSITY PRESS

CAMBRIDGE UNIVERSITY PRESS
Cambridge, New York, Melbourne, Madrid, Cape Town,
Singapore, São Paulo, Delhi, Tokyo, Mexico City

Cambridge University Press
32 Avenue of the Americas, New York, NY 10013-2473, USA

www.cambridge.org
Information on this title: www.cambridge.org/9780521127516

First published 2012

Printed in Hong Kong, China, by Golden Cup Printing Company Limited

A catalog record for this publication is available from the British Library.

ISBN 978-0-521-12755-4 Student's Book 3 with Self-study CD-ROM
ISBN 978-0-521-12751-6 Workbook 3
ISBN 978-0-521-12747-9 Teacher's Edition 3 with Assessment Audio CD / CD-ROM
ISBN 978-0-521-12743-1 Class Audio CDs 3
ISBN 978-0-521-12712-7 Classware 3
ISBN 978-0-521-12740-0 DVD 3

For a full list of components, visit www.cambridge.org/fourcorners

Art direction, book design, photo research, and layout services: Adventure House, NYC

سرشناسه: ریچاردز، جک کرافت، ۱۹٤۳- م.
Richards, Jack Croft
Four Corners 3: Workbook/Jack C. Richards, David Bohlke, with Kathryn O'dell.
عنوان و نام پدیدآور:
مشخصات نشر: تهران: رهنما، ۱۳۹۱= ۲۰۱۲ م.
مشخصات ظاهری: ۹۹ ص.؛ ۲۲ × ۲۹ س.م.
وضعیت فهرست‌نویسی: فیپا
یادداشت: انگلیسی
یادداشت: افست از روی چاپ ۲۰۱۲م: Cambridge University Press
آوانویسی عنوان: فور کرنرز ...
موضوع: زبان انگلیسی - - کتاب‌های درسی برای خارجیان
موضوع: زبان انگلیسی - - مسائل، تمرین‌ها و غیره
شناسه افزوده: بولک، دیوید
شناسه افزوده: Bohlke, David
شناسه افزوده: اودل، کاترین ال.
شناسه افزوده: O'Dell, Kathryn L
ردهبندی کنگره: ۱۳۹۱ ٤۹۷ ٨۳ف PE۱۱۲٨/
ردهبندی دیویی: ٤۲٨/۲٤
شماره کتابشناسی ملی: ۲۹٦٨٥٠٨

مؤلفین: Jack C. Richards & David Bohlke، لیتوگرافی: رهنما، چاپ: چاپخانه نقره‌فام، چاپ اول: ۱۳۹۱، تیراژ: ۵۰۰۰ نسخه، Four Corners 3 Workbook
ناشر: انتشارات رهنما، آدرس: مقابل دانشگاه تهران، خیابان فروردین، نبش خیابان شهدای ژاندارمری، پلاک ۱۱۲، تلفن: ۶۶٤۰۰۹۲۷، ۶۶٤۱۶۶۰٤، ۶۶٤٨۱۶۶۲، فاکس: ۶۶٤۶۷٤۲٤
فروشگاه رهنما، سعادت‌آباد، خیابان علامه طباطبایی جنوبی، بین ٤۰ و ٤۲ شرقی پلاک ۲۹، تلفن: ۸۸۶۹٤۱۰۲، آدرس فروشگاه شماره ٤: خیابان پیروزی نبش خیابان سوم نیروی
هوایی، تلفن: ۷۷٤٨۲۵۰۵، نمایشگاه کتاب رهنما، مقابل دانشگاه تهران پاساژ فروزنده، تلفن: ۶۶۹۵۰۹۵۷

قیمت: ۴۵۰۰۰ ریال

Contents

Credits

Illustration credits

Kveta Jelinek: 1, 9, 47, 62, 73; Andrew Joyner: 12, 20, 45, 50; Greg Paprocki: 4, 10, 21, 36, 46, 55, 70, 77; Garry Parsons: 5, 14, 22, 25, 49, 71; Maria Rabinky: 33, 93; Rob Schuster: 76; Richard Williams: 23, 29, 68, 75

Photography credits

6 ©Gulf Images/Alamy; 8 ©Media Bakery; 11 ©Juice Images/Alamy; 16 ©Michele Falzone/Alamy; 17 (clockwise from top left) ©Eva Mueller/Getty Images; ©Dorling Kindersley/Getty Images; ©Zee/Alamy; ©RT Images/Alamy; ©Shutterstock; ©Shutterstock; ©Siri Stafford/Getty Images; ©Ghislain & Marie David de Lossy/Getty Images; 18 ©Hulton Archive/Getty Images; 20 (top to bottom) ©Shutterstock; ©Kirsty McLaren/Alamy; 23 ©Media Bakery; 24 (top to bottom) ©Hulton Archive/Getty Images; ©Archive Photos/Getty Images; ©Ryan Miller/Getty Images; 26 ©Media Bakery; 28 ©Dreamstime; 30 (top to bottom) ©Media Bakery; ©Image Broker/Alamy; 32 ©Tyler Stableford/Aurora/Getty Images; 34 ©Asia Images/Getty Images; 35 (left to right) ©Hisham Ibrahim/Getty Images; ©Laura Ciapponi/Getty Images; 37 (clockwise from top left) ©Media Bakery; ©Paul Souders/Getty Images; ©Altrendo Travel/Getty Images; ©Media Bakery; ©Shutterstock; ©Oliver Strewe/Getty Images; 38 ©Media Bakery; 39 ©Image Makers/Getty Images; 40 (left to right) ©Doug Armand/Getty Images; ©Steve Bloom Images/Alamy; ©Philip & Karen Smith/Getty Images; 41 ©Ty Milford/Getty Images; 48 (top to bottom) ©Shutterstock; ©Tony Cordoza/Getty Images; ©Jack Hollingsworth/Getty Images; ©Jeffrey Coolidge/Getty Images; 51 ©Mike Powell/Getty Images; 52 (top to bottom) ©Iain Masterton/Alamy; ©Rene Magritte/Bridgeman Art Library/Superstock; ©Charles Stirling/Alamy; ©Oleksiy Maksymenko/Alamy; 57 (clockwise from top left) ©Media Bakery; ©Marlene Ford/Alamy; ©Franz Aberham/Getty Images; 60 ©Alamy; 61 (clockwise from top left) ©Justin Prenton/Alamy; ©Photo Library; ©Media Bakery; ©Media Bakery; ©Photo Library; ©Media Bakery; 63 (top to bottom) ©Fuse/Getty Images; ©Media Bakery; ©Fancy/Alamy; ©Media Bakery; ©Media Bakery; ©Media Bakery; 64 ©Media Bakery; 69 ©Media Bakery; 74 ©Tomás del Amo/Alamy; 79 (left to right) ©Ian Miles – Flashpoint Pictures/Alamy; ©Magdalena Rehova/Alamy; ©Media Bakery; (bottom) ©Tyler Stableford/Getty Images; 82 ©Redferns/Getty Images; 84 ©Frederick Bass/Getty Images; 87 ©Jason LaVeris/Getty Images; 89 (clockwise from top left) ©Jay Reilly/Getty Images; ©Media Bakery; ©Wendy Connett/Alamy; ©Alamy; 90 ©Nicolas Russell/Getty Images; 92 ©Photo Edit; 94 ©Alamy; 96 (left to right) ©Shutterstock; ©Shutterstock; ©Theo Fitzhugh/Alamy; ©Creative Crop/Getty Images; ©Creative Crop/Getty Images

Education

A I'm taking six classes.

1 Look at the pictures. Write the correct school subjects.

1. c<u>hemistry</u>

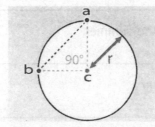
2. g_____

3. w_____

      g_____

4. m_____

5. h_____

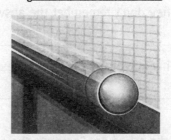
6. p_____

7. b_____

8. a_____

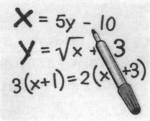
9. a_____

2 Complete the sentences with the correct school subjects from Exercise 1.

1. Sandra's favorite classes are science classes: _____*chemistry*_____ ,
_____ , and _____ .

2. John has two math classes: _____ and _____ .

3. Leo's favorite classes are in the arts: _____ and _____ .

4. Mi-hee is taking two social studies classes: _____
and _____ .

3 Check (✓) the correct sentences. Rewrite the incorrect sentences with the correct forms of the verbs. Use the simple present or the present continuous.

1. ☐ Dina reads her email right now.

   Dina is reading her email right now.

2. ☐ Tim is knowing a lot about biology.

   _____

3. ☐ Mary and Alicia are taking a swimming class together.

   _____

4. ☐ I'm wanting to study in Australia in the summer.

   _____

5. ☐ What is the word "engineer" meaning?

   _____

6. ☐ Do you go to class right now?

   _____

7. ☐ They don't remember the answers for the history test.

   _____

8. ☐ This homework isn't seeming difficult.

   _____

4 Look at the schedule. Complete the sentences with the correct forms of *work*. Use the simple present or the present continuous.

Officemart Summer Schedule			
Name	**Fridays**	**Saturdays**	**Sundays**
Marcia	2:00 p.m. – 8:00 p.m.	9:00 a.m. – 3:00 p.m.	✗
Leo	10:00 a.m. – 5:00 p.m.	9:00 a.m. – 5:00 p.m.	12:00 p.m. – 4:00 p.m.
Paul	✗	2:00 p.m. – 7:30 p.m.	✗

1. Marcia and Leo _____*work*_____ on Fridays and Saturdays.

2. It's Sunday, and Marcia and Paul _____ .

3. It's 11:00 a.m. on Friday. Leo _____ .

4. It's 3:30 p.m. on Saturday. Leo and Paul _____ right now.

5. Leo _____ on Sunday afternoons.

6. Paul _____ on Fridays.

7. It's 6:00 p.m. on Friday. Leo _____ right now.

8. Marcia and Leo _____ on Saturday evenings.

5 Complete the text messages with the correct forms of the verbs in parentheses.
Use the simple present or the present continuous.

J.Monk78: Hi, Shelly. What _are you doing_____ (do) right now?
                                              1

SLP1980: Hey, Jin-sung. I _____ (write) to you! 😊
                              2

J.Monk78: Very funny! _____ you _____ (study) for the chemistry test?
                          3   3

SLP1980: Yes, I am. Linda and I _____ (read) the teacher's notes online.
                                    4

J.Monk78: I _____ (not / understand) those notes at all.
               5

SLP1980: _____ you _____ (want) some help?
             6   6

J.Monk78: Yes, please!

Emmie: Hey, Kate. What classes _____ you _____ (have) on Fridays?
                                   7   7

KateM: I _____ (have) algebra in the mornings and geometry in the afternoons.
             8

Emmie: What time _____ (be) your geometry class?
                     9

KateM: At 2:00. Wait . . . my sister _____ (call) me . . .
                                         10

KateM: OK. I'm back. My sister _____ (shop) right now. Let's go to the mall.
                                   11

Emmie: OK, but I _____ (work) right now. How about at 11:30?
                     12

KateM: Great! Let's meet in front of Los Zapatos Shoe Store.

---

6 Answer the questions with your own information. Write complete sentences.

Example: _I'm taking English, physics, and music._

1. What classes are you taking? _____

2. When do you study? _____

3. How often do you have English classes? _____

4. Where do you usually do your homework? _____

5. What school subjects do you like? _____

6. What school subjects do you hate? _____

7. What are you doing right now? _____

8. Where are you sitting? _____

B You're not allowed to . . .

1 Complete the chart with the sentences from the box.

> ✓ You can't use your cell phone in the office.   You need to have lunch at that time.
> You have to come to work by 9:00.   You're not permitted to eat in your office.
> You must always wear a suit to work.   You're not allowed to write emails to friends.

Prohibition	Obligation
You can't use your cell phone in the office.	

2 Complete the conversation with the correct sentences from the box in Exercise 1.

Ms. Jones: Welcome to Akron Accounting. This is your new office. Do you have any questions?

Mr. Okada: Yes. Can I make personal phone calls at work?

Ms. Jones: No, I'm sorry. <u>*You can't use your cell phone in the office.*</u>
1
You can make personal calls at lunch.

Mr. Okada: OK. What time is lunch?

Ms. Jones: It's from 1:00 to 2:00.

_____
2

Mr. Okada: Can I have lunch at my desk?

Ms. Jones: No, I'm sorry. _____ .
3
You can have lunch in our café, or you can go out to eat. There are a lot of good restaurants on Pine Street.

Mr. Okada: OK. Thanks. Is there anything else I need to know?

Ms. Jones: Yes. _____ .
4
We try to dress for business here.

Mr. Okada: No problem.

C My behavior

1 Look at the pictures. Complete the puzzle with the feelings and emotions you see.
What's the mystery word?

1.

2.

3.

	¹T	H	I	R	S	T	Y	
	²							
3								
4								
5								
6								

4.

5.

6.

2 Complete the sentences with the correct words from the box.

| hungry   jealous   scared   ✓ thirsty   upset |

1. Miguel wants some water. He's _____ _thirsty_ _____ .

2. Carla didn't eat lunch today, and now she's very _____ .

3. John's team didn't win their soccer game. He's extremely _____
   about it.

4. Paula is an actress. Mariana wants to be an actress, but right now she's a waitress.
   She's _____ of Paula.

5. When Peggy came home last night, her front door was open. She was
   _____ and called the police.

3 Complete the conversation with *if* and the correct words from the box.

I have a job interview	I'm prepared	there's a website
I'm nervous	she's home	✓you're nervous

Carmen: Hey, Danielle. What do you do

if you're nervous ?
        1

Danielle: _____ about
                2

something, I try not to think about it.

Carmen: Well, I have a job interview tomorrow, and

I have to think about it!

Danielle: Hmm . . . _____ ,
                        3

I usually prepare before I go. It really helps.

Carmen: How do you prepare?

Danielle: _____ , I read about the place online.
                4

Carmen: That's a good idea.

Danielle: Yes. I also practice the interview with my sister _____ .
                                                                    5

Carmen: I can try that with my brother. What about during the interview?

Danielle: _____ , I usually don't get nervous. Good luck!
                6

4 Combine the sentences into one. Use *when*. Write it in two ways.

1. Emma has a test. → She studies a lot.

   When Emma has a test, she studies a lot.

   Emma studies a lot when she has a test.

2. I get bad news. → I get upset.

   _____

   _____

3. Jordan gets up early in the morning. → He is sleepy.

   _____

   _____

4. My sister is busy. → She doesn't call me.

   _____

   _____

5. Lorena and Jessie have a soccer game. → They get nervous.

   _____

   _____

5 Write sentences in the zero conditional. Use the words in the chart.

Condition	Main clause	If / When
1. Tonya's sister / go to a party	Tonya / always / get jealous	when
2. Greg / be lonely	he / often / call a friend	when
3. I / get scared	I / always / call my brother	if
4. Kyle and Rick / be busy	they / sometimes / not eat	if
5. Leticia / get angry	she / usually / not say anything	when
6. I / be late for work	I / usually / say I'm sorry	if

1. _When Tonya's sister goes to a party, Tonya always gets jealous._

2. _____

3. _____

4. _____

5. _____

6. _____

6 Write questions with the words in parentheses. Use *What* and the zero conditional.

1. (Charlie / do / if / be sleepy)   _What does Charlie do if he's sleepy?_

2. (you / do / when / get upset)   _____

3. (Frank and Julie / do / if / get angry) _____

4. (you / do / if / be hungry)   _____

5. (you and your friends / do / when / be thirsty) _____

6. (Annette / do / when / feel nervous)   _____

7 Answer the questions with your own information. Write complete sentences with the zero conditional.

Example: _When I'm nervous about a test, I study really hard._

1. What do you do when you're nervous about a test? _____

2. What do you do if you're sleepy in class? _____

3. How do you feel when you're too busy? _____

4. What do you do when you're lonely? _____

5. What do you drink if you're thirsty? _____

6. What do you say when you're angry with a friend? _____

D Alternative education

1 Read the article. Answer the questions.

1. Who works for a magazine? _____

2. Who works for an engineer? _____

Work-Study Programs in High School

Many high schools in the United States have work-study programs. In their last year of high school, some students have a job for part of the day as one of their "classes." Some of these students make money and some don't, but all of them learn important things about having a job and being a good worker. Many people think that when students learn outside of the classroom in a real job, they prepare for life after high school. Work-study programs can really help students get a job or get into college.

There are many types of work-study programs. Most of the students work in offices, but not all of them do. Some students fix cars, and others work outside with environmental engineers. Big businesses, like computer companies and banks, often work with high schools to create work-study opportunities for students as well.

Raul Gomez usually goes to school from 9:00 a.m. to 4:00 p.m., but this year he works for a magazine from 7:00 a.m. to 11:00 a.m. He says, "I learn important things in my work-study program. I must be at work on time. And if I miss a day, they don't pay me!" At work, he reads stories and fixes spelling and grammar mistakes. He says, "At work, I use what I learn in my English class. And now I think that someday, I might want to write for a magazine or a newspaper."

Raul Gomez at his work-study job

Annie Miller works for an engineer in her work-study program. They design and help make bridges, roads, and buildings. She says, "It's great! I love learning math in school, but at work, I use algebra and geometry in the real world!"

Not all high schools offer work-study programs. But most of the schools that have them think they are a big success.

2 Read the text again. Then write T (true), F (false), or NI (no information).

1. Work-study programs started in the United States. __*NI*__

2. Some students get money in work-study programs. _____

3. Work-study programs rarely help students start their careers or further their education. _____

4. Raul works at his job in the morning. _____

5. Annie likes science classes. _____

6. Not many of the work-study programs are a success. _____

Personal stories

A *What were you doing?*

1 Put the letters in the correct order to make adverbs. Complete the sentences.

(y u o u t r n l f t a n e)

1. I was having a great day on Tuesday. Then, ___*unfortunately*___ , I left my bag at a restaurant.

(l l i c y u k)

2. _____ , someone found it.

(l y f e t o a n u t r)

3. And _____ , my cell phone was in the bag.

(l s y r u i n s g i p r)

4. _____ , the person who found it called my home phone.

David !

(a z n i g a y m l)

5. _____ , the person was David, a boy I went to school with when I was six! We made plans to meet at a café.

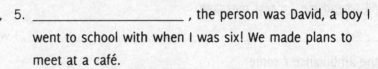

(y e s t a r g l n)

6. _____ , David looked the same! We ate lunch and talked a lot.

(s n u e y d d l)

7. Then David got a phone call, and he left the café _____ .

(s a y l d)

8. _____ , I never saw him again.

2 What were they doing when the lights went out? Write sentences with the past continuous forms of the verbs.

1. (Mi-na / read / a book)

   Mi-na was reading a book.

2. (Martin / wash / the dishes)

   _____

3. (Brad and Kate / watch / TV)

   _____

4. (I / talk / to Tom / on the phone)

   _____

5. (Laura / play / video games)

   _____

6. (Mr. and Mrs. Jones / eat / dinner)

   _____

3 Complete the sentences with *when* and the words in parentheses.
Use the simple past forms of the verbs.

1. (their friends / arrive)

   Jane and Paul were making dinner on Friday _*when their friends arrived*_____ .

2. (his brother / call)

   Martin was driving to the store _____ .

3. (the electricity / go off)

   What were you doing yesterday _____ ?

4. (Jill / send me / a text message)

   _____ , I was talking to Tom on my cell phone.

5. (the ambulance / come)

   What were they doing _____ ?

6. (the storm / begin)

   _____ , I was walking home from work.

4 Complete the conversation with the correct forms of the simple past or the past continuous of the verbs in parentheses.

Rick: Hi, Lisa. What _____*were*_____ you _____*doing*_____ (do)
                                    1
        when the electricity _____*went*_____ (go) off?
                                        2

Lisa: Unfortunately, I _____ (work)
                                    3
        on the computer! I couldn't finish my work. What

        _____ you _____ (do)?
                4   4

Rick: Oh, I _____ (sleep) when
                        5
        everything _____ (go) dark.
                            6
        I didn't even know what happened.

Lisa: Really? It was only 7:30 p.m.

Rick: Well, I _____ (take) a nap in the living room. I think I slept
                        7
        for a long time. When I _____ (wake) up, it was really dark.
                                        8
        So I just went to bed. While everyone _____ (have) problems,
                                                            9
        I _____ (sleep)!
                10

5 Complete the story with the verbs in the box. Use the past continuous or the simple past.

✓cook	go	make	stand	turn
fall	hear	see	try	

Terry and Wendy _____*were cooking*_____ in the kitchen when the electricity suddenly
                            1
_____ off. Unfortunately, while Terry _____ to find
        2   3
a light, he _____ down. He _____ a loud noise.
                    4   5
When Wendy _____ the noise, she _____ by the
                    6   7
window. While she _____ around, she _____
                            8   9
something move outside the window. What was it?

6 Answer the questions with your own information. Write complete sentences.

Example: _I took biology, history of China, and English last year._

1. What classes did you take last year? _____

2. What were you saying the last time you spoke? _____

3. Where did you eat breakfast today? _____

4. What did you do last night? _____

5. What were you doing at 6:00 a.m. today? _____

6. What were you doing when class started? _____

Guess what!

1 Write **A** (announcing news) or **C** (closing a conversation).

1. Listen, I've got to run. ___C___

2. You'll never guess what happened! _____

3. Sorry, I have to go. _____

4. Hey, I need to get going. _____

5. Guess what! _____

6. Did you hear what happened? _____

2 Complete the conversations with the sentences from Exercise 1. Sometimes more than one answer is possible. Use each sentence once.

A. **Jim:** Hello, Pat. *Did you hear what*
   happened?
   ₁

   Pat: No, I didn't.

   Jim: There was an accident on Main Street.

   Pat: That's terrible!

   Jim: Yes, it is. Fortunately, everyone is OK.
   _____ .
   ₂

   Pat: OK. Bye.

a car accident

B. **Annie:** Hey, Tonya! _____ !
   ₁

   Tonya: What?

   Annie: Martin got a promotion, and he's moving to Canada.

   Tonya: That's great.

   Annie: I know. _____ . I have a meeting
   ₂
   in a few minutes.

   Tonya: No problem. Call me later!

C. **Beth:** Hi, Dan. _____ !
   ₁

   Dan: What?

   Beth: Our soccer team won the competition.

   Dan: That's fantastic! _____ . I have
   ₂
   class now. But congratulations!

   Beth: That's OK. Thanks. See you tomorrow.

C I was really frightened!

1 Put the letters in the correct order to make verbs that describe reactions.

1. i e t e c x _____*excite*_____
2. d u s s g i t _____
3. s o u n f c e _____
4. i t t n r s e e _____
5. g e t h f i r n _____
6. a u e s m _____
7. e c n l a g h l e _____
8. s m a e s a r b r _____

2 Complete the conversations with the correct forms of the verbs in Exercise 1. Use the simple present.

1. **Nancy:** Hey, Karl. Did you do the homework for math class?

   Karl: No, I didn't. Geometry _____*confuses*_____ me. I don't understand it.

2. **Po:** Jill. Try this sushi.

   Jill: No, thanks. Fish _____ me! I hate it!

3. **Larry:** My brother talks too loudly. He really _____ me when he's with my friends.

   David: It's not so bad. He's very friendly.

4. **Tom:** What _____ you, Seth?

   Seth: Horror movies! I get really scared when I watch them.

5. **Ted:** Do you like animated movies?

   Lea: Yes, they usually _____ me. I think they're funny.

6. **Ahmet:** Chemistry _____ me, but I think physics is boring.

   Andrea: Really? I think physics is interesting.

7. **Miho:** What do you want to do this weekend? Anything exciting?

   Karen: Well, the idea of going to Chicago for the weekend _____ me!

8. **Eva:** You're pretty good at sports, Tim. What kind of sport _____ you?

   Tim: Golf, I guess. It's a lot more difficult than it seems.

3 Complete the sentences with the present participles (*-ing*) or past participles (*-ed*) of the verbs in parentheses.

1. Amusement parks are _____*exciting*_____ (excite).

2. Can you help me? This physics problem is _____ (confuse).

3. I want a new job because my work is too easy. I don't feel _____ (challenge).

4. I don't think your problem is _____ (embarrass). A lot of people talk fast when they're nervous.

5. I'm _____ (frighten) by our neighbor's dog! It's big and extremely loud.

6. I'm not _____ (interest) in math, but I love science.

7. I don't think video games are _____ (amuse), but many teenagers like them.

8. My brother is _____ (disgust) by reality shows, but I'd like to be on one!

4 Circle the correct words to complete the conversation.

Paul: Hi, Wendy. Have you ever read *Life of Pi*? You know . . . that story about a boy who is on the ocean in a boat with a tiger.

Wendy: Yes, I have. I liked it, but I thought some parts with the tiger were **disgusted** / **(disgusting)**. 1

Paul: Really? I thought it was **frightened** / **frightening**, 2 but I was **excited** / **exciting** when I read it. 3

Wendy: Well, yes, it was **excited** / **exciting**. But after a 4 while, I think Pi was probably **bored** / **boring** on 5 that boat. He was on it for 227 days!

Paul: Oh, I don't think so. I bet life on that boat wasn't **bored** / **boring** at all! I loved how he became friends with the tiger. That was 6 really **interested** / **interesting**. 7

Wendy: Yeah. That part was **amused** / **amusing**, I guess, but it didn't seem like real life. 8

Paul: Maybe not, but I think the story shows that sometimes life is **challenged** / **challenging**. 9

Wendy: Yeah, you're right. And I guess the end was **surprised** / **surprising**. 10

Paul: Um, well . . . now I'm **embarrassed** / **embarrassing**. To be honest, I didn't 11 finish the book!

5 Read Ron's online survey. Then complete the sentences about Ron's opinions.

```
◄ ► C  [                                    ]        ⊖ ⊗

  We want to hear from you!

  1  What kind of music are you interested in?
     ☑ pop      ☐ country  ☐ gospel   ☑ classical
  2  What do you think of concert ?
     ☑ exciting   ☐ boring    ☑ amusing
  3  Who are you embarrassed by?
     ☐ your parents    ☑ your brothers and sisters   ☐ your friends
  4  What do think about technology?
     ☑ confusing   ☑ challenging   ☐ easy
  5  What kinds of foods do you think are disgusting?
     ☑ fish     ☐ meat     ☐ fruit    ☑ vegetables
```

1. Ron is _____*interested*_____ in _*pop and classical music*_____ .

2. He thinks _____*concerts*_____ are _____ .

3. He is _____ by _____ .

4. He thinks _____ is _____ .

5. He thinks _____ are _____ .

6 Write sentences about your opinions with a participial adjective from the box.

Example: _I think horror movies are amusing._ or _I'm frightened by horror movies._

amused / amusing	disgusted / disgusting	frightened / frightening
bored / boring	embarrassed / embarrassing	interested / interesting
challenged / challenging	excited / exciting	surprised / surprising
confused / confusing		

1. horror movies: _____

2. history classes: _____

3. the news: _____

4. reading books: _____

5. reality shows: _____

6. math: _____

D How embarrassing!

1 Read the email. Then check (✓) the correct adjectives.

1. The hotel is _____ .

☐ interesting   ☐ dirty   ☐ embarrassing

2. The Japanese street names are _____ .

☐ amusing   ☐ challenging   ☐ disgusting

3. Angela did two things that were _____ .

☐ traditional   ☐ interesting   ☐ embarrassing

Hi George,

I'm having an amazing time in Japan! I'm in Kyoto visiting a lot of interesting places. I'm staying in a *ryokan*. It's a traditional Japanese hotel. It's really interesting. The hotel is part of a man and woman's home. Their names are Mr. and Mrs. Ito. I have breakfast by myself at the *ryokan*, and I eat lunch in the city, but I have dinner with the family in their part of the house. And their daughter brings me tea in the evening before I go to bed! (I feel like a very important person!)

I'm learning a lot about life in Japan, but I'm also doing some embarrassing things by mistake! In the *ryokan*, you take off your shoes before you go in the house so that the floor doesn't get dirty. You leave your shoes outside the door. On my first day, I took off my shoes, but I did it in my bedroom. I walked through the house first, and I got the floor dirty. How embarrassing! I hope Mr. and Mrs. Ito weren't disgusted with me. But they are nice and very friendly, and now I remember to take off my shoes before I come in the house.

I was also embarrassed while I was traveling around the city yesterday. I don't speak Japanese, but I speak Spanish. When I asked for directions, no one understood me! I was pronouncing the street names like Spanish words. They're very difficult to say! But it's easy to get around in Kyoto. The buses and trains are extremely modern and clean. Tomorrow I'm going to an art museum. I'm going to practice pronouncing the museum name and the street name in Japanese tonight!

It's really fun here. I don't want to go back home!

Your friend,

Angela

---

2 Read the text again. Then answer the questions. Write complete sentences.

1. Where is Angela staying in Kyoto? _____

2. Who gives Angela tea? _____

3. What two embarrassing things did Angela do? _____

4. What is Angela's opinion of the buses and trains? _____

5. What is Angela doing tomorrow? _____

Style and fashion

A Fashion trends

1 Look at the pictures. Complete the puzzle with fashion words.

Across

4.

5.

7.

8.

Down

1.

2.

3.

6.

2 Cross out the fashion word that doesn't belong in each list.

1. **Clothing:** ~~a bracelet~~ a leather jacket a uniform

2. **Hairstyles:** a ponytail dyed hair sandals

3. **Jewelry:** earrings a bracelet glasses

4. **Eyewear:** contact lenses earrings glasses

5. **Shoes:** sandals a uniform high heels

3 Put the words in the correct order to make sentences.

1. high heels / to work / used / I / to / wear / .

   I used to wear high heels to work.

2. wear / used / to / wig / My / mother / a / .

   _____

3. every / Jason / day / use / didn't / wear / suits / to / .

   _____

4. to / lenses / have / contact / Did / use / you / ?

   _____

5. on vacation / We / used / buy / to / T-shirts / .

   _____

6. to / Katia / Did / use / wear / earrings / big / ?

   _____

7. dyed / to / didn't / Sandra / and Bethany / use / have / hair / .

   _____

8. used / a / My / to / ponytail / daughter / have / long / .

   _____

4 Circle the correct words to complete each conversation.

1. **A:** Did you _____ to have dyed hair?

   B: No, I _____ , but I do now.

   a. use, did   (b.) use, didn't   c. used, did   d. used, didn't

2. **A:** Did Leo _____ to wear a bracelet?

   B: Yes, he _____ ! But now he doesn't wear any jewelry.

   a. used, did   b. used, didn't   c. use, did   d. use, didn't

3. **A:** Where _____ Kelly and Margie use to shop?

   B: They _____ to shop at the mall.

   a. didn't, use   b. didn't, used   c. did, use   d. did, used

4. **A:** What kinds of clothes did Jake _____ to wear?

   B: He _____ to wear T-shirts and baggy jeans.

   a. use, use   b. used, use   c. use, used   d. used, used

5. **A:** Did you _____ to wear glasses?

   B: Yes. I didn't _____ to wear contact lenses.

   a. use, use   b. used, use   c. use, used   d. used, used

5 Look at Emma's information. Then write sentences with the words in parentheses. Use *used to* or *didn't use to*.

What did you use to wear?	1970s	1980s	1990s	2000s
baggy jeans	✓	X	X	✓
tight jeans	X	✓	✓	✓
bright T-shirts	✓	✓	X	X
high heels	X	X	✓	✓
big earrings	✓	✓	✓	X

1. (bright T-shirts / the 1970s)   *Emma used to wear bright T-shirts in the 1970s.*

2. (high heels / the 1970s)   *She didn't* _____

3. (baggy jeans / the 1980s) _____

4. (tight jeans / the 1980s) _____

5. (big earrings / the 1990s) _____

6. (big earrings / the 2000s) _____

B Does this come in . . . ?

1 Write the conversation in the correct order.

> Can I help you?
> ✓ Excuse me.
> No, I'm sorry. It only comes in black.
>
> Oh, thanks! Um, do you have this in brown?
> They're here, behind you.
> Yes. Where can I find the leather jackets?

Renaldo: _Excuse me._

Clerk: _____

Renaldo: _____

Clerk: _____

Renaldo: _____

Clerk: _____

2 Write a conversation for each picture with the words in the box and your own ideas. Use the conversation in Exercise 1 as a model.

> Can I get this in . . . ?
> Could you tell me where the . . . are?
>
> Does this come in . . . ?
> Where are the . . . ?

1. **Debbie:** Excuse me.

   Clerk: _____ ?

   Debbie: Yes. _____ ?

   Clerk: _____ .

   Debbie: Oh, thanks! _____ in red?

   Clerk: No, I'm sorry. _____ .

2. **Ichiro:** _____ .

   Clerk: _____ ?

   Ichiro: Yes. _____ ?

   Clerk: _____ .

   Ichiro: Oh, thanks! _____ in blue?

   Clerk: Yes. _____ .

20 Unit 3 Lesson B

C The latest look

1 Read about the types of clothes. Then write the fashion word that matches each type.

1. clothes that people like right now but might not like next year: <u>t r e n d y</u>

2. clothes that are the style that people want or like: __ __ __ __ __ __ __ __ __ __ __ __

3. clothes that used to be what people liked: __ __ __ - __ __ __ __ __ __ __ __ __

4. new clothes that look like old styles (in a good way): __ __ __ __ __

5. clothes that look expensive and exciting (in a good way): __ __ __ __ __ __ __ __ __ __

6. usually cheap clothes of bad quality or bad style: __ __ __ __ __

7. clothes that look very strange: __ __ __ __ __

8. clothes that attract a lot of attention because they're bright: __ __ __ __ __ __

2 Look at the pictures. Complete the sentences with your own opinions. Use words from the box. Not all the words will be used.

fashionable	glamorous	retro	trendy
flashy	old-fashioned	tacky	weird

Example: <u>*Her dress is fashionable.*</u> or <u>*Her dress is flashy.*</u>

1. Her dress is _____ .

2. Her shoes are _____ .

3. Her sunglasses are _____ .

4. His shirt is _____ .

5. His pants are _____ .

6. His hat is _____ .

3 Rewrite the sentences. Replace *that* with *which* or *who*.

1. I don't like clothes that are trendy.

   I don't like clothes which are trendy.

2. Tonya is the kind of person that buys things for other people.

   _____

3. I like the kind of store that has a lot of sales.

   _____

4. Is Jason someone that follows fashion trends?

   _____

5. We prefer salesclerks that give us their opinions.

   _____

6. Carla prefers shoes that are not high heels.

   _____

7. Is there a store in the mall that sells sunglasses?

   _____

8. Greg and Roberto are people that always wear retro clothes.

   _____

4 Complete the conversation with *which* or *who*.

Emily: Mom, what is a fashion designer?

Mom: It's a person _____ who _____ makes new
   clothing styles.
              1

Emily: And what is a tailor shop?

Mom: It's a store _____ has tailors.
                    2

Emily: OK . . . but what's a tailor?

Mom: Well, a tailor is a person _____
                                   3
   makes or fixes clothes.

Emily: Really? OK. And what does a stylist do?

Mom: That's a person _____ helps actors look good.
                        4

Emily: Thanks, Mom!

Mom: Why are you asking me all these questions?

Emily: I found this magazine _____ is about fashion. I'm taking a quiz in it.
                                5

Mom: You mean, *I'm* taking a quiz in it!

5 Read the question. Then complete the response with *who, that,* or *which* and the correct forms of the verbs and other words in parentheses.

1. **A:** Who is Ms. Young?

   B: She is the chemistry teacher _who wears_
      flashy clothes . (wear / flashy clothes)

2. **A:** Does Marvin buy all types of clothes?

   B: No, he doesn't. He usually buys clothes

      _____ .

      (be / fashionable)

3. **A:** What kind of malls do you like?

   B: I like malls _____ .
      (have / a lot of stores with trendy clothes)

4. **A:** Who is Jennifer X?

   B: She's a singer _____ .
      (wear / weird clothes at her concerts)

5. **A:** Who is Jacques?

   B: He's that famous designer _____ .
      (make / retro clothing)

6. **A:** What is *Viv?*

   B: It's a website _____ .
      (sell / old-fashioned jewelry)

6 Complete the sentences with your own information.

Example: _Black is a color that I wear a lot._

1. _____ is a color that I wear a lot.

2. _____ is a person who has a style that I really like.

3. _____ is a magazine or website that people read
   for information about style.

4. _____ is a clothing style that is trendy right now.

5. _____ is a place that sells clothes that I like
   to wear.

6. _____ is someone who wears clothes that are
   stylish.

1 Read the article. Then match the two parts of each sentence.

1. Coco Chanel was a woman _____   a. who made the first jeans.

2. Levi Strauss was the man _____   b. who wrote about style.

3. Richard Blackwell was a person _____   c. who designed hats and clothing for women.

People Who Changed Clothing Style

Coco Chanel was a French designer who changed style for women. She started making glamorous hats in her apartment. Then a famous actress wore Chanel's hats in a play, and suddenly many women wanted her hats. So Chanel started a business and opened a hat store in 1913. In the early 1900s, women used to wear uncomfortable skirts, but Chanel wanted to be comfortable. She often wore men's pants, jackets, and ties. She started making comfortable and stylish clothing for women. She made pants and women's suits that were comfortable and trendy, and she began selling them in her store. By 1919, she opened a larger store and was famous in France and other parts of the world. She changed women's clothing, and she inspired other designers.

Levi Strauss had a clothing store in California in the 1870s. His store sold work clothes for men. At that time, working men wore pants that ripped or tore a lot. Strauss worked together with the tailor Jacob Davis to make better pants that were strong and that a man could wear for a long time. They made the pants with a heavy cloth called denim. At that time, there was another heavy cloth called jean. People started to call the denim pants *jeans*. Jeans used to be for work, but they became trendy in the 1950s when teenagers started wearing them. Now many people wear them, even when they aren't working.

Richard Blackwell was an American designer who wrote about style. In 1960, he wrote a "Ten Worst-Dressed Women" list in a magazine. People didn't use to talk badly about famous people's clothes, but Blackwell wrote about actresses who wore clothes that he thought were ugly or weird. Today, there are many TV shows with people who give opinions about the clothes that actors and actresses are wearing these days. There are also many websites that have "Worst-Dressed" lists about celebrities.

2 Read the article again. Answer the questions. Write complete sentences.

1. What was the first item of clothing Coco Chanel made?   *She made hats.*_____

2. Why did Chanel sometimes wear men's clothing?   _____

3. Why did Levi Strauss make pants from denim?   _____

4. Who made jeans trendy?   _____

5. Who did Richard Blackwell write about?   _____

Interesting lives

A Have you ever been on TV?

1 Look at the pictures. Check (✓) the correct sentence for each picture.

1. ☑ I often get seasick.
   ☐ I often lose my phone.
   ☐ I often win an award.

2. ☐ I moved to a new city last week.
   ☐ I was on TV last week.
   ☐ I acted in a play last week.

3. ☐ I met a famous person in New York.
   ☐ I broke my arm in New York.
   ☐ I was on TV in New York.

Excellence in Business

4. ☐ I got seasick at work.
   ☐ I broke my arm at work.
   ☐ I won an award at work.

5. ☐ I used to act in plays.
   ☐ I used to be on TV.
   ☐ I used to win awards.

6. ☐ We're meeting a famous person.
   ☐ We're acting in a play.
   ☐ We're moving to a new city.

2 Complete the chart. Write the past participles. Then write R (regular) or I (irregular).

Base Form	Past Participle	Regular or Irregular
1. lose		
2. be		
3. act		
4. chat		
5. see		
6. win		
7. have		
8. go		

Base Form	Past Participle	Regular or Irregular
9. try		
10. break		
11. happen		
12. do		
13. meet		
14. move		
15. eat		
16. get		

3 Complete the conversation with the present perfect forms of the verbs in parentheses. For answers to questions, use short answers.

Joe: Hey, Marta. _____*Have*_____ you ever
                          ¹
    _____*been*_____ (be) on TV?
                  ¹

Marta: Yes, I _____*have*_____ . I was interviewed
                    ²
    about the Japanese language school I went to
    in Tokyo. Hey, _____ you ever
                         ³
    _____ (visit) Japan?
           ³

Joe: No, I _____ .
                ⁴

Marta: It's great. I studied there for a month.

Joe: What did you like the best?

Marta: The food! _____ you ever _____ (try) sushi?
                    ⁵   ⁵

Joe: Yes, I _____ . I like Japanese food. I also like Korean
                ⁶
    food. _____ you ever _____ (try) Korean food?
                ⁷   ⁷

Marta: Yes. I _____ . A few times. _____ you ever
                ⁸   ⁹
    _____ (go) to South Korea?
         ⁹

Joe: No, I _____ . But my sister _____ (be) there. She went to Seoul.
              ¹⁰   ¹¹

Marta: I hear they have good food at the markets in Seoul. _____ she ever
                                              ¹²
    _____ (eat) at a night market?
          ¹²

Joe: Yes, she _____ . She _____ (have) food at
                ¹³   ¹⁴
    night markets lots of times.

Marta: That's cool!

4 Look at the chart. Then write questions and short answers with the words in parentheses. Use the present perfect.

What have you done?						
	play table tennis	do karate	break a bone	act in a play	be on TV	chat online
Emily	✓			✓		✓
Ken		✓	✓			✓
Sandra		✓		✓		✓
Marcos		✓		✓	✓	✓
Julia	✓			✓		

1. (Emily / break a bone)

   Question: _Has Emily ever broken a bone_ ? Answer: _No, she hasn't_ .

2. (Emily and Ken / be on TV)

   Q: _____ ? A: _____ .

3. (Ken / play table tennis)

   Q: _____ ? A: _____ .

4. (Sandra / do karate)

   Q: _____ ? A: _____ .

5. (Marcos / chat online)

   Q: _____ ? A: _____ .

6. (Marcos and Julia / act in a play)

   Q: _____ ? A: _____ .

5 Look at the chart in Exercise 4. Write sentences about what you have and haven't done. Use *never* for negative sentences.

Example: _I've played table tennis lots of times._

I've never done karate.

1. _____

2. _____

3. _____

4. _____

5. _____

6. _____

B What I mean is, . . .

1 Cross out the expression that doesn't belong in each list.

1. Are you saying . . .   Do you mean . . .   What I mean is, . . .

2. Do you mean . . .   What I'm saying is, . . .   I mean . . .

3. What I mean is, . . .   Does that mean . . .   What I'm saying is, . . .

4. What I'm saying is, . . .   Does that mean . . .   Do you mean . . .

5. Does that mean . . .   I mean . . .   Are you saying . . .

6. What I'm saying is, . . .   Are you saying . . .   What I mean is, . . .

2 Circle the correct words to complete the conversation.

Jenny: I'm really sleepy.

Amy: Really? Why?

Jenny: I didn't sleep last night.

Amy: (Do you mean)/ I mean you didn't get any sleep?
        1

an alarm clock

Jenny: Well, no. **What I mean is, / Does that mean** I didn't get *much* sleep.
                        2

Amy: That's too bad. It was better for me. I couldn't stay awake!

Jenny: **What I'm saying is, / Are you saying** that you slept a lot?
                            3

Amy: Well, yes. **I mean / Do you mean** I slept all night . . . for about eight hours.
                    4

Jenny: Oh. What time do you usually go to bed?

Amy: I go to bed about 10:00 p.m., and I never use an alarm clock in the morning.

Jenny: **What I mean is, / Does that mean** you get up late in the morning?
                    5

Amy: No. . . . **What I'm saying is, / Are you saying** I wake up early. I always wake up
                            6
        at 6:00 a.m. I don't need an alarm.

Jenny: That's nice. I never wake up early without an alarm.

C Life experiences

1 Look at the pictures of Roger and Mary's trip. Then complete the email with the correct expressions from the box.

| climbed a mountain | tried an extreme sport | went to a spa |
| tried an exotic food | ✓ went camping | went whale-watching |

1.

2.

3.

4.

5.

6.

Hi Lorena and Bill,

We're having a lot of fun in Canada with our friends. Victoria is a beautiful city. Last weekend we

___*went camping*___ near the ocean. It was great. We
        1

_____ on Saturday, and we _____
      2   3

on Sunday. Roger and I even _____ : zip-lining. You go through the
                                  4

air from tree to tree! It was exciting!

This week, we're staying in a nice hotel. We had dinner at a very nice restaurant in the hotel last

night. I _____ . I ate broiled rainbow trout with fiddleheads and rice.
                 5

Rainbow trout is a delicious fish. Fiddleheads are an exotic vegetable. I even

_____ at the hotel with Barbara. Can you believe it? It was very
                 6

relaxing. Roger and Tim didn't go.

I have to say good-bye now. We're going to an amusement park in Vancouver, a big city near

Victoria. I can't wait to ride the roller coasters!

Write soon,

Mary

2 Complete the sentences with the correct forms of the words in parentheses. Use the present perfect or the simple past.

1. I *'ve been* _____ (be) to Mexico lots of times.

2. My sister _____ (eat) at a Turkish restaurant yesterday.

3. Paulina _____ (never / go) to a spa, but I _____ (go) to one last month.

4. _____ you ever _____ (try) an extreme sport?

5. I _____ (try) skiing last year, but I _____ (not / like) it.

6. _____ Jorge and Vanessa _____ (ride) a roller coaster at the park yesterday?

7. What countries _____ you _____ (be) to in the past?

8. My cousins _____ (go) camping last week, but I _____ (never / go) camping before.

3 Write questions to complete the conversations. Use the present perfect and the simple past.

A. **Hyun-ju:** Hey, Matt. *Have you ever gone camping* _____ ?
           ₁

  Matt: No, I haven't. But my sister went camping last weekend.

  Hyun-ju: Really? _____ ?
               ₂

  Matt: Yes, she did. She had a lot of fun.

  Hyun-ju: _____ ?
               ₃

  Matt: No. She didn't climb a mountain, but she went kayaking.

  Hyun-ju: Wow! _____ ?
               ₄

  Matt: No, I have never gone kayaking. But I'd like to go sometime.

  Hyun-ju: Me too!

B. **Josh:** How was your vacation, Nicky?

  Nicky: It was great! _____ ?
             ₁

  Josh: No, I didn't get your postcard. _____ ?
            ₂

  Nicky: I sent it on Monday. It's from Mexico City.

  Josh: Cool!

  Nicky: _____ ?
             ₃

  Josh: Yes, I have. I went to Mexico City last year.

  Nicky: _____ ?
             ₄

  Josh: Yes, I saw the pyramids. They were amazing!

  Nicky: Great! You're going to like my postcard!

4 Look at the chart. Write sentences about what Victor has done using the information in the chart. Use the present perfect or the simple past.

	never	last year	a few years ago	lots of times
1. bowl		✓		
2. play golf			✓	
3. do yoga	✓			
4. join a gym			✓	
5. lift weights				✓
6. climb a mountain	✓			
7. play soccer				✓
8. try karate		✓		

1. _Victor bowled last year._
2. _He_
3. _____
4. _____
5. _____
6. _____
7. _____
8. _____

5 Answer the questions with your own information. Write complete sentences. If your answer is no, add more information.

Example: _Yes, I have. I found it on the beach._ or
         No, I haven't. I don't take my phone on vacation.

1. Have you ever lost your phone on vacation? If yes, did you find it?

_____

2. Did you go on vacation last year? If yes, where did you go?

_____

3. Have you ever tried an extreme sport? If yes, did you like it?

_____

4. Have you ever won an award? If yes, why did you win it?

_____

5. Have you ever met a famous person? If yes, who did you meet?

_____

6. Have you ever gotten seasick? If yes, where were you?

_____

D *What a life!*

1 Read the article. Write the correct question from the box before each answer.

Is it dangerous?   Are *caving* and *spelunking* different?   What is spelunking?

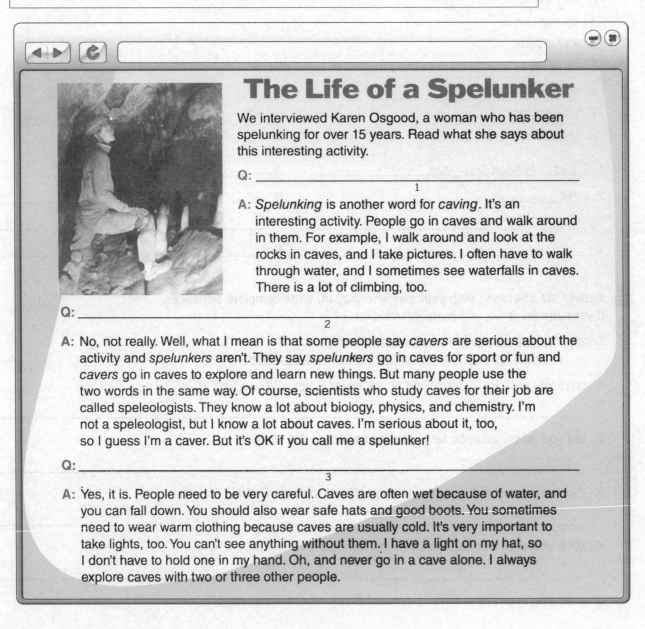

The Life of a Spelunker

We interviewed Karen Osgood, a woman who has been spelunking for over 15 years. Read what she says about this interesting activity.

Q: _____
                              1

A: *Spelunking* is another word for *caving*. It's an interesting activity. People go in caves and walk around in them. For example, I walk around and look at the rocks in caves, and I take pictures. I often have to walk through water, and I sometimes see waterfalls in caves. There is a lot of climbing, too.

Q: _____
                              2

A: No, not really. Well, what I mean is that some people say *cavers* are serious about the activity and *spelunkers* aren't. They say *spelunkers* go in caves for sport or fun and *cavers* go in caves to explore and learn new things. But many people use the two words in the same way. Of course, scientists who study caves for their job are called speleologists. They know a lot about biology, physics, and chemistry. I'm not a speleologist, but I know a lot about caves. I'm serious about it, too, so I guess I'm a caver. But it's OK if you call me a spelunker!

Q: _____
                              3

A: Yes, it is. People need to be very careful. Caves are often wet because of water, and you can fall down. You should also wear safe hats and good boots. You sometimes need to wear warm clothing because caves are usually cold. It's very important to take lights, too. You can't see anything without them. I have a light on my hat, so I don't have to hold one in my hand. Oh, and never go in a cave alone. I always explore caves with two or three other people.

2 Read the article again. Then write T (true) or F (false).

1. Karen has been spelunking for many years. ___*T*___

2. People don't climb in caves. _____

3. There's sometimes water in caves. _____

4. Spelunkers study caves as part of their job. _____

5. There isn't a lot of light in caves. _____

6. You should always go caving with other people. _____

Our world

A Older, taller, and more famous

1 Label the things in the picture with the correct words.

1. c<u>anal</u>
2. b_____
3. tu_____

4. p_____
5. su_____
   sy_____

6. to_____
7. sk_____
8. st_____

2 Put the words in the correct order to make sentences.

1. is / the Akashi-Kaikyo Bridge in Japan / older / The Tower Bridge in England / than / .

   The Tower Bridge in England is older than the Akashi-Kaikyo Bridge in Japan.

2. the Erie Canal in the United States / than / is / The Murray Canal in Canada / shorter / .

   _____

3. more / The Sydney Harbor Bridge in Australia / is / than / modern / the Tower Bridge in England / .

   _____

4. as / long / the Channel Tunnel between England and France / The Lincoln Tunnel between New Jersey and New York City / is / not / as / .

   _____

5. tall / the Sears Tower in the United States / is / The Jin Mao Tower in China / not / as / as / .

   _____

6. the London Underground / people on it / has / The New York City subway system / more / than / .

   _____

7. as / as / large / the Zócalo square in Mexico City / is / The Plaza Mayor in Madrid / not / .

   _____

3 Circle the correct words to complete the paragraphs.

There are many skyscrapers in Hong Kong. Two very tall skyscrapers
are the Bank of China Tower and Central Plaza. Central Plaza is
more tall than / **taller than** the Bank of China Tower. It also has
    1
more floors than / **more floors** the Bank of China Tower. The Bank
    2
of China Tower is **older than** / **older** Central Plaza. But it looks
    3
more modern / **more modern than** Central Plaza.
    4

I. M. Pei created the Bank of China Tower, and Dennis Lau and Ng
Chun Man created Central Plaza. Some people say that I. M. Pei has
created **more famous buildings than** / **more than famous buildings**
    5
Dennis Lau and Ng Chun Man. He has made buildings around the
world. For example, he made the John F. Kennedy Library in Boston
and the pyramid at the Louvre Museum in Paris.

| Bank of China Tower | Central Plaza |

4 Read about the bridges. Then write comparisons with the words in parentheses. Use -er endings or more . . . than.

The Brooklyn Bridge, New York City   The Golden Gate Bridge, San Francisco

1. The Brooklyn Bridge is 1,825 meters long. The Golden Gate Bridge is 2,737 meters long. (is / long)

   The Golden Gate Bridge is longer than the Brooklyn Bridge.

2. The Brooklyn Bridge is 26 meters wide. The Golden Gate Bridge is 27 meters wide. (is / wide)

   _____

3. The Brooklyn Bridge opened in 1883. The Golden Gate Bridge opened in 1937. (is / old)

   _____

4. The cost to build the Brooklyn Bridge was $15.5 million. The Golden Gate Bridge was $35 million. (was / expensive)

   _____

5. It took 13 years to build the Brooklyn Bridge. It took four years to build the Golden Gate Bridge. (took / time to build)

   _____

6. Each day, 145,000 people go on the Brooklyn Bridge. Each day, 118,000 people go on the Golden Gate Bridge. (has / people on it each day)

   _____

5 Change sentences 1–4 from Exercise 3. Use not as . . . as.

1. *The Brooklyn Bridge is not as long as the Golden Gate Bridge.*

2. _____

3. _____

4. _____

1 Complete the conversation. Use expressions for expressing disbelief and for saying you don't know. The first letter of each word is given.

Tyler: Hey, Susana, look at this.

Susana: What is it?

Tyler: It's information about the plazas in Mexico. There are more plazas in Mexico than anywhere else in the world!

Susana: *I don't believe it!* _____

1

Tyler: And we're in a very famous plaza – the Zócalo. Do you know another name for it?

Susana: I h_____ n_____ i_____ .

2

Tyler: It's also called Constitution Plaza.

Susana: That's interesting. But I like the name Zócalo better. . . . How old is it?

Tyler: I r_____ d_____ k_____ . But the plaza is older than

3
some of the buildings around it.

Susana: S_____ ?

4

Tyler: Yeah. There used to be different buildings around the plaza, but over the years people built new buildings in place of some of the old ones.

Susana: N_____ w_____ ! I wonder why the old ones are gone. . . .

5
Hey, do you know how big the square is?

Tyler: It says here it's 240 meters long and 240 meters wide.

Susana: That's pretty big! Hey, I'm hungry. Is there a restaurant near the plaza?

Tyler: I d_____ h_____ a c_____ ! Maybe there are some

6
ideas in this book.

2 Complete the conversations with one of the expressions from Exercise 1. More than one answer is possible.

1. **A:** Do you know how long the Channel Tunnel is?

   B: _____

2. **A:** Wow! Did you know the Weihe Grand Bridge is the longest bridge in the world?

   B: _____

C *World geography*

1 Complete the puzzle with words for geographical features. What's the mystery word?

1.   2.   3.

4.   5.   6.

¹R I V E R

2

3

4

5

6

2 Complete the sentences with words for geographical features.

1. The Nile _____*River*_____ is 6,650 kilometers long.

2. A _____ is extremely dry and hot.

3. We swam in a small _____ on vacation.

4. The Indian _____ has less water than the Atlantic or Pacific.

5. Maui is a beautiful _____ surrounded by the Pacific Ocean.

6. I went to the Amazon _____ _____ last winter.
   The trees and other plants were beautiful, and I saw a lot of animals, but it
   really rained a lot!

7. When we went camping last summer, we put up our tent in a _____
   next to a river. Every morning, we looked up at the mountains all around us. It was great!

8. The most famous _____ in the United States is Niagara Falls.

3 Complete the text with the correct superlative forms of the adjectives in parentheses.

YOSEMITE NATIONAL PARK

Yosemite National Park is one of ___*the most beautiful*___ (beautiful)
parks in the United States, and it's one of _____
(large) parks in California. There are many interesting geographical
features in Yosemite. Yosemite Valley is _____
(popular) place to visit in the park. It's easy to walk around in the
valley. Tuolumne River is _____ (long) river in the
park, and there are many river trips you can take. There are also many
waterfalls to see in the park. Yosemite Falls is _____ (high) waterfall.
Chilnualna Falls is one of _____ (difficult) to see because it's behind rocks.

January, February, and March are _____ (wet) months in Yosemite. Spring
is _____ (good) season to see waterfalls. Summer is
_____ (hot) season, and it's also the _____ (busy)
season. There aren't many visitors in the park in the winter because it's very cold.

4 Look at the chart. Write sentences with superlative nouns.

In the Caribbean			
	Aruba	**Cuba**	**the Dominican Republic**
1. land	180 km²	110,860 km²	48,670 km²
2. people	104,589	11,477,459	9,794,487
3. rain (each year)	21.3 inches	52 inches	54.5 inches
4. official languages	2	1	1
5. TV stations	1	58	25

1. ___*Cuba has the most land.*___
2. _____
3. _____
4. _____
5. _____

5 Complete the sentences with the superlative forms of the underlined words.

1. **A:** We're going to New Guinea this year. It's an extremely large island.

   B: Yes, it is. But Greenland is *the largest* island in the world.

2. **A:** This street has a lot of cars. Is there always this much traffic?

   B: Yes, First Avenue gets *the most traffic* in the city.

3. **A:** My uncle does research in the Antarctic Desert, and he says it's really cold.

   B: I know. The Antarctic Desert is _____ desert in the world.

4. **A:** What a great day! Let's sit in the sunshine.

   B: OK. This is _____ we've had all summer!

5. **A:** Wow, this is beautiful! We're up so high. What a great view!

   B: Did you know Lake Titicaca is one of _____ lakes in the world?

6. **A:** I'm going to Japan. Where is a good place to see temples?

   B: I think Kyoto is one of _____ places to see temples in Japan.

7. **A:** I'm tired of being wet on this vacation! It has rained every day on this trip.

   B: Well, May is usually _____ month in this city.

8. **A:** How many people live in New York?

   B: Over 8 million. It's the city in the United States with _____ .

Greenland

6 Answer the questions with your own information. Write complete sentences and use superlatives.

Example: *The longest bridge I've ever been on is the Golden Gate Bridge.*

1. What's the longest bridge you've ever been on? _____

2. Where's the highest place you've ever been? _____

3. What's the most beautiful place you've ever seen? _____

4. Where's the hottest place you've ever been? _____

5. What's the tallest building in your town? _____

6. What's the longest river in your country? _____

7. Which city in your country has the most people? _____

8. Which month gets the most rain in your town? _____

Natural wonders

1 Read the article. Then write the name of the correct natural wonder under each picture.

1. _____ 2. _____ 3. _____

Canada's Seven Wonders

In 2007, the CBC TV and radio stations had a contest to choose the Seven Wonders of Canada.
People sent their ideas to a website and voted for their favorites.

People's Choices	Votes
Sleeping Giant: This is a long peninsula in Lake Superior, which means it has water on three sides. From across the lake, it looks like a big, sleeping person!	177,305
Niagara Falls: These amazing waterfalls are on the border of Canada and the United States. There are three waterfalls, but the largest and most beautiful is called Horseshoe Falls, and most of it is in Canada.	81,818
Bay of Fundy: This is a large body of water where the Atlantic Ocean meets part of Canada. It has the highest tides in the world. The water from the ocean comes in 17 meters higher than when it goes out!	67,670
Nahanni National Park Reserve: This beautiful national park in northern Canada has rivers, waterfalls, mountains, forests, birds, fish, and other animals.	64,920
Northern Lights: These are colorful moving lights in the sky. The best time to see them is on very dark, cool nights in March, April, September, and October.	61,417
The Rockies: The Canadian Rockies are beautiful, high mountains that have sharp peaks and wide valleys. They are cool and wet, but the tops have no trees because it is too cold and rocky for them to grow.	55,630
Cabot Trail: This 950-kilometer hiking trail through part of the Rockies has some of the most beautiful views in Canada. It is named after John Cabot, an Italian man who explored the land in 1497.	44,073

2 Read the article again. Then answer the questions.

1. When was the contest for the Seven Wonders of Canada? _____ *2007* _____

2. Which place had the most votes? _____

3. Which ocean's water goes into the Bay of Fundy? _____

4. What are the best months to see the northern lights? _____

5. How long is the Cabot Trail? _____

Organizing your time

A A busy week

1 Complete the phone conversations with words from the box.

✓birthday	business	doctor's	soccer
meeting	conference	job	violin

A. **Jake:** Hey, Ramon. Can you come to my

_____*birthday*_____ party on Saturday?

1

Ramon: I'm not sure. I have a _____

2

appointment at the hospital at 2:00 p.m. What

time is the party?

Jake: It starts at 4:00 p.m. And there's someone

I want you to meet. His name is Mark.

Ramon: Well, I can come to the party. But I don't know about Mark. I've never

been on a _____ with him.

3

Jake: You're both just going to be at the party. It'll be fun!

B. **Yae-jih:** Hi, Don. How are you?

Don: OK. I'm a little nervous about my _____ interview at TGL Bank.

1

Yae-jih: Oh, right. When is it?

Don: Today at 2:00. Mr. Lawrence and Mrs. Nelson have a lot of _____

2

meetings, so we are going to have a _____ call. I won't have an

3

interview face-to-face.

Yae-jih: Wow. That's different. Good luck!

C. **Laura:** Hello, Sibel. Do you want to have lunch tomorrow?

Sibel: I'm sorry. I can't. I have a _____ lesson tomorrow.

1

How about on Saturday?

Laura: I have _____ practice in the afternoon.

2

Let's have dinner on Saturday night.

Sibel: OK, great. And we can go to a movie after dinner, too.

2 Circle the correct words to complete the email.

Hi Jim,

How are you? Thanks for your email. It will be great to see you next week. What
(are you doing) / **do you do** on Thursday? I have tickets to a pop concert, if you'd
1
like to go with me. **It's starting** / **It starts** at 8:00 p.m. **I'm having** / **I have** soccer
2   3
practice at 4:00, but **it's ending** / **it ends** at 5:30. If you can go to the concert, we could
4
meet for dinner at 6:30 at Oh Boy Pizza. What do you think?

Are you busy on July 28th? **I'm moving** / **I move** that day. Could you help me move?
5
Katie and Mike **are helping** / **help** me, too. They **are going** / **go** to a yoga class every
6   7
Saturday from 8:00 to 10:00 a.m., so we'll start at 11:00. **I'm buying** / **I buy** lunch for
8
everyone.

I hope you can go to the concert. Write soon or call me!

Raul

3 Check (✓) the correct sentences. Rewrite the incorrect sentences with the correct forms
of the verbs. Use the simple present or the present continuous.

1. ☐ Lorena is having a violin lesson every Thursday.

   Lorena has a violin lesson every Thursday.

2. ☐ Do you have any doctor's appointments next week?

   _____

3. ☐ Marvin picks up his sister in Miami at 3:30 p.m. on Saturday.

   _____

4. ☐ Brenda and Tom are staying at my house this weekend.

   _____

5. ☐ Naoki plans a conference call in meeting room B for Tuesday next week.

   _____

6. ☐ The movie starts at 9:00 and is ending at 11:30.

   _____

4 Read the sentences. Check (✓) if the event is happening right now or in the future.

	Now	Future
1. I can't have lunch now. I'm studying for my biology test.	☑	☐
2. I have a doctor's appointment on Friday.	☐	☐
3. Jen is working late next week.	☐	☐
4. I'm eating a great sandwich. Do you want to try it?	☐	☐
5. I'm sorry. Tae Jung isn't here. He has soccer practice.	☐	☐
6. Melanie can't go on a blind date on Saturday. She has a guitar lesson.	☐	☐
7. We're leaving for vacation in three days!	☐	☐
8. Larry isn't answering his cell phone. He is on a conference call.	☐	☐

5 Complete the calendar with your own plans for next week. Write sentences with the present continuous or the simple present.

Example: Sunday: _I have gymnastics practice._ or _I'm visiting my aunt and uncle._

WEEKLY CALENDAR

Sunday	
Monday	
Tuesday	
Wednesday	
Thursday	
Friday	
Saturday	

B *Can I take a message?*

1 Put the words in the correct order to make sentences for leaving and offering to take phone messages.

1. leave / want / a / message / to / you / Do / ? _Do you want to leave a message?_

2. Amber called / him / Please / tell / that / . _____

3. is at 12:15 / the conference call / her / Can / you / tell / that / ? _____

4. know / in the morning / that / you / her / Could / let / we're leaving / ? _____

5. like / to / you / Would / leave / message / a / ? _____

6. take / a / message / I / Can / ? _____

2 Complete the conversations with sentences from Exercise 1. Each sentence in Exercise 1 is used once. Sometimes, the first word is given.

A. Brandon: Hello?

   Amber: Hi. Can I speak to Jim?

   Brandon: I'm sorry. He's not here. Do
     you want to leave a message ?
     ₁

   Amber: Sure. _____
                 ₂
     _____ .

> **While You Were Out**
>
> **For:** _Jim_   **Date:** _October 2_
>
> **Message:** _Amber called._
>
> _909-555-1234_
>
> _____
>
> _____

B. Victoria: Hello?

   Marcos: Hello. Can I speak to Tonya, please?

   Victoria: Um, she's busy right now. Can _____ ?
                              ₁

   Marcos: Yes. We have a business meeting at work tomorrow.
     _____ ?
              ₂

   Victoria: 12:15. OK. No problem.

C. Emma: Hello?

   Asami: Hi. Is Kendra there?

   Emma: No, she isn't. Would _____ ?
                        ₁

   Asami: Oh, sure. I'm picking her up tomorrow for a camping trip.
     _____ ?
              ₂

   Emma: OK. What time?

   Asami: About 10:00 a.m.

C Can you do me a favor?

1 Circle the correct phrase to complete each conversation.

1. **A:** Algebra is difficult.

   B: Do you want some help?

   A: Yes. Can you **help me with my résumé /** check my homework?

2. **A:** That restaurant is too expensive.

   B: I know, but the food is really good. Let's go.

   A: Well, OK. Could you **lend me some money / water my plants?**

3. **A:** Hi, Ed. It's Sherry.

   B: Hi, Sherry. You're calling me early. Is there a problem?

   A: Yes. My car isn't working. Can you **check my homework / give me a ride to work?**

4. **A:** Look at those flowers! Your garden is so beautiful!

   B: Thanks. Would you mind **watering the plants / getting the mail** with me?

5. **A:** Julia is so nice. She always wants to help.

   B: I know. She's **feeding my cat / giving me a ride** while I'm on vacation.

6. **A:** Do you want to go to a movie tonight?

   B: I'm sorry, I can't. I'm **getting my mail / picking up my parents at the airport.**

7. **A:** I need to find a job.

   B: My office needs some new workers.

   A: Really? That's great. Could you **help me with my résumé / pick me up?**

8. **A:** Does anyone stay at your house when you travel for work?

   B: No. My neighbor usually **gets my mail / checks my homework.**
   And he also feeds my fish.

2 Complete the conversation with words from the box.

✓ can you do	I'll clean	I won't forget	would you mind cleaning
could you take	I'll cook	Would you make	

Tina: Matt, _can you do_____ me a favor?
1

Matt: Sure, Tina. What is it?

Tina: I'm going to be home late tonight, around 7:00.

_____ dinner?
2

Matt: No problem. _____ tacos
3

and rice and beans.

Tina: Oh, that sounds great! And _____
4

_____ out the garbage? It has to go out tonight.

Matt: Definitely. _____ . I promise!
5

Tina: Thanks. Oh, and _____ the apartment? Our new
6

neighbors, Jay and Camille, are coming over for dinner. Remember?

Matt: Um, OK. I guess _____ it before I make dinner.
7

Tina: Thanks. You're the best!

3 Rewrite the questions. Use *would you mind*. Then complete the responses with *will*.

1. Can you check my homework?

   A: _Would you mind checking my homework?_

   B: No problem. _I'll check_____ it after dinner.

2. Could you pick me up at 10:30 a.m.?

   A: _____

   B: Not at all. _____ at any time you want me to.

3. Would you give me a ride to my doctor's appointment?

   A: _____

   B: No problem. _____ you a ride in my new car!

4. Would you tell Josh that the meeting is tomorrow?

   A: _____

   B: No, I don't mind. _____ him when I see him at lunch.

5. Could you water the plant in my office while I'm out next week?

   A: _____

   B: No problem. _____ it. How often should I do it?

4 Look at Eric's notes. Then complete his conversation with each person.

1. **Eric:** Can you give me a ride to the airport on Monday afternoon?

   Priscilla: No problem. *I'll give you a ride to the airport.* What time?

give me a ride to the airport	Priscilla
feed my fish	Chuck
feed my cat	Chuck
get my mail	Amira
pick me up from the airport	Greg

2. **Eric:** Can _____
   while I'm on a trip next week?

   Chuck: Sure. _____ them.

   Eric: And would you mind _____ , too?

   Chuck: No, I don't mind. _____ it, too.

3. **Eric:** Would _____ when I'm on my trip?

   Amira: All right. _____ it on Wednesday and Friday.

4. **Eric:** Could _____ at 4:30 on Sunday?

   Greg: Yeah, sure. _____ and
   _____ be late!

5 People are asking you favors. Write their questions and your own answers.

1. **Ed:** *Can you take my picture* ?

   You: _____ .

2. **Mai:** _____ ?

   You: _____ .

3. **Chris:** _____ ?

   You: _____ .

4. **Mara:** _____ ?

   You: _____ .

D Time management

1 Read the article. What are four ways that people waste time?

1. _the Internet_   2. _____   3. _____   4. _____

A Waste of Time!

Many people don't manage their time well. They often find other things to do when they should be working. Some people don't even know they are wasting time. These are some of the top time-wasters. Do any of them sound like you?

1. The Internet is a very useful tool, but it's also the biggest way people waste time. Many people play games or chat online instead of working or doing research for school. Have you ever looked at a funny video online instead of working?

2. TV can be interesting and educational, but many people waste time by watching TV. Have you ever taken a short break from work to watch "just a little TV" and then hours later thought, "Oh, that's right. . . . I was doing laundry."?

3. People can actually waste a lot of time when they talk. At work, some people talk too much about personal things instead of doing their jobs. Other people have the same problem at home. They talk to friends and family on the phone instead of doing chores.

4. Believe it or not, thinking can be a waste of time. Some people think about work, but they don't do it. They even make to-do lists, but then they just think about all the things they have to do, and they never get them done!

2 Read the article again and the sentences below. Did each person waste time? Check (✓) Yes or No.

	Yes	No
1. Vicky researched information on the Internet for a work report.	☐	☑
2. Dan played a game online for two hours at work.	☐	☐
3. Ines watched TV for ten minutes and then finished her homework.	☐	☐
4. Haluk talked to his boss about a business meeting.	☐	☐
5. Sam talked to his boss about his son's soccer game.	☐	☐
6. Jen made a to-do list, and then she thought about how she'd never finish all of it.	☐	☐

Personalities

A *You're extremely curious.*

1 Put the letters in the correct order to make words for personality traits.

1. i a t s m i u b o   _ambitious_
2. b n s u b r t o   _____
3. e a c f l r u   _____
4. i o c m i t t i s p   _____

5. r s c i u u o   _____
6. o t i g u g o n   _____
7. u d s r t o n u a e v   _____
8. a i e o y n g s g   _____

2 Complete the sentences with the words for personality traits.

John sets high goals for himself. He's very

_____ _ambitious_ _____ . He's also extremely

              1

_____ . He loves learning

              2
about new things.

Celia is _____ , but she's also

              3

pretty _____ . She likes trying

           4
exciting sports, but she does them with attention
to detail.

Gina doesn't have a job right now, but she seems
OK. She always looks on the bright side, so she's

_____ about her future. She

         5
hardly ever worries. She's a very relaxed and

_____ person.

       6

Daniel can be very _____ .

             7
He never changes his mind about things! But

he's also very _____ .

            8
He's extremely friendly, so people like to be
around him.

3 Circle the correct words to complete the conversation.

Jane: How do your children like college, Rob?

Rob: Very much, thanks. Don is **carefully** / (**extremely**)
1
ambitious. He sets high goals for himself. You
know, he wants to be a pilot.

Jane: Wow. That's great. And the others?

Rob: Well, Greg **fairly** / **really** likes college. He's
2
early / **very** outgoing. He works **early** / **well** in
3   4
groups, but he thinks it's difficult to work alone, and you have do that a lot in college.

Jane: Well, it's good that he likes school.

Rob: And Ken is **pretty** / **slowly** curious. He likes to learn new things, so he loves school.
5
He's interested in many subjects, so he hasn't decided what career he wants yet.

Jane: That sounds like my son. And how's Brandon doing?

Rob: He's doing OK. He doesn't work **very** / **well** without direction, but if you tell him
6
what to do, he does it **really** / **well**. Ken and Brandon go to the same college,
7
so they help each other.

Jane: That's nice.

4 Rewrite the sentences to correct the mistakes in the order of the words.
Sometimes there is more than one mistake in the sentence.

1. Steven and Susan are curious extremely about the new student in class.

    Steven and Susan are extremely curious about the new student in class.

2. Mario doesn't play well the guitar when he's nervous.

   _____

3. Tae-ho's parents are important very to him.

   _____

4. Kendra is outgoing fairly, and she makes easily new friends.

   _____

5. Pam quickly drives, but she's careful pretty.

   _____

6. Jacob slowly is moving, so he'll be late for his doctor's appointment this morning.

   _____

5 Look at the chart. Write sentences about Shan.

	easily	very	fairly	hard
1. make friends	✓			
2. ambitious			✓	
3. study during the week				✓
4. not stubborn		✓		
5. not work on the weekends				✓
6. outgoing		✓		
7. optimistic			✓	
8. not share her feelings	✓			

1. *Shan makes friends easily.* _____

2. *She is* _____

3. _____

4. _____

5. _____

6. _____

7. _____

8. _____

6 Complete the sentences so they are true for you. Use some of the adverbs from the box.

Example: *I'm pretty ambitious.* or *I'm not very ambitious.*

carefully	(not) extremely	pretty	slowly
completely	fairly	quickly	(not) very
easily	hard	(not) really	well

1. I'm _____ ambitious.

2. I'm _____ serious about learning English.

3. I'm _____ optimistic about my future.

4. I make new friends _____ .

5. I'm _____ curious about math and science.

6. I work _____ when I do my homework.

B In my opinion, . . .

1 Complete the conversations with phrases from the box. Use each expression once.
More than one answer is possible.

Don't you agree	Don't you think that's true	In my opinion,
Don't you think so	If you ask me,	Maybe it's just me, but I think

Olivia: Heather, what do you think of this statue?

Heather: Oh, it's very interesting. _Don't you agree_ ?

1

Olivia: No, not really. _____ it's ugly.

2

Olivia: And look at this painting. What do you think of it?

Heather: I like it, but it's a little weird. _____ ?

3

Olivia: _____ it's pretty amazing!

4

Olivia: Wow. Look at this. It's great! _____ ?

5

Heather: No, I don't. _____ it's disgusting!

6

2 What do you think? Complete the conversation with your own idea. Use an expression
for giving an opinion.

Olivia: Hey, what do you think of this painting?

Heather: Oh, it's nice. Don't you agree?

You: _____

_____

_____

C

We've been friends for six years.

1 Look at the dictionary definitions for personality traits. Write the correct words.

1. a _greeable_____ (adj) friendly and pleasing

2. c_____ (adj) thinking of the needs of others

3. d_____ (adj) making decisions quickly

4. f_____ (adj) treating people equally or right

5. h_____ (adj) truthful

6. m_____ (adj) behaving in a responsible way

7. p_____ (adj) waiting without getting annoyed

8. r_____ (adj) doing what is expected or promised

2 Complete the sentences with the correct words for personality traits.
Use the opposites of the words from Exercise 1.

1. John is sometimes _____ _dishonest_____ . He doesn't always tell the truth.

2. Some people in the group were _____ , so we didn't become friends.

3. Jack is pretty _____ . He didn't come to pick me up at the airport.
   I had to take a taxi home.

4. Amanda is 17, but she's pretty _____ . She acts like she's only
   12 or 13.

5. Please don't be _____ ! You don't have to wait much longer. I'm
   almost finished.

6. Bob and I are often _____ . We hardly ever make decisions quickly!

7. Peter is a very _____ and _____ person.
   He never thinks about other people's needs, and he doesn't treat people equally.

3 Complete the chart. Write the words from the box in the correct column.

✓2010	a few days	last night	two months
4:30	five hours	a long time	Wednesday
December	I was 18	quite a while	a year

I've lived here for . . .	I've known him since . . .
_____	_____2010_____
_____	_____
_____	_____
_____	_____
_____	_____

4 Look at the calendar and the information about Vanessa. Today is Saturday.
Complete the sentences with *since*. Then rewrite them with *for*.

Monday	Tuesday	Wednesday	Thursday	Friday
got a new job	met Greg at work	had a blind date with Carlos	stopped talking to Greg	got sick

1. Vanessa has had a new job *since Monday*_____ .

   *Vanessa has had a new job for five days.*_____

2. She has known Greg _____ .

   _____

3. She has known Carlos _____ .

   _____

4. She's hasn't talked to Greg _____ .

   _____

5. She's been sick _____ .

   _____

5 Write sentences with the words in parentheses. Use the present perfect with *for* or *since*.

1. (Yolanda / be / friends with Jenna / a long time)

   Yolanda has been friends with Jenna for a long time.

2. (I / not see / Jun / three days)

   _____

3. (I / not have / an argument with my parents / I was a kid)

   _____

4. (Tom and Melissa / be / married / three years)

   _____

5. (Matt / not eat / sushi / he was in Japan)

   _____

6. (Sandra / know / Katia / 2005)

   _____

6 Read the email. Then answer the questions. Use *for* or *since*.

Dear Uncle Henry,

How are you? I'm great! As you know, I got married a week ago! I'm sorry you couldn't come to the wedding. Can you believe that I met Julie at your son's wedding in 2001?

Julie and I are on vacation now. We got to Hawaii four days ago. It's beautiful here! Unfortunately, Julie got sick on Wednesday, so we're in the doctor's office now. We got here at 1:00 p.m., and we have to wait a little longer to see the doctor. The office is pretty busy. Julie's mother called five minutes ago, and they're talking on the phone now. Julie's going to be OK. She probably had some bad seafood.

I have to go. They say I have to turn off my computer!

Take care,

Josh

1. How long has Josh been married?   _He's been married for a week._

2. How long has Josh known Julie?   _____

3. How long have Josh and Julie been in Hawaii?   _____

4. How long has Julie been sick?   _____

5. How long have they been in the doctor's office?   _____

6. How long has Julie been on the phone?   _____

D   *What is your personality?*

1 **Read the article. Then answer the questions.**

1. Which color in the article do you like best? _____

2. Are you like (or not like) the personality description for that color? _____

What does your favorite color say about your personality?

We all have a favorite color. But did you know that your favorite color might say something about your personality?

WHITE. White is a peaceful color. You like simple things. You are extremely fair, and you always tell the truth. You also want your friends to be truthful.

RED. Red is a strong color. You are outgoing and like meeting new people. You are optimistic and very ambitious. You are also decisive, and you are sometimes stubborn.

ORANGE. You are pretty easygoing and you like to be agreeable. You are curious about people and like to learn about them. You have a lot of friends. You want people to notice you, and you sometimes dress in flashy clothes!

YELLOW. Yellow is a happy color. You are very funny and have a lot of friends. You are pretty adventurous, too! But

sometimes you are not very responsible. That's not always a bad thing because taking risks is fun if you are careful.

GREEN. Green is the color of nature. You're fairly curious about the world. You like to be outdoors, and you are also adventurous. You are patient, kind, and easygoing.

BLUE. Blue is also a color in nature. Like "green" people, you are also very patient. You are reliable, and you want your friends to be considerate. You probably aren't very adventurous.

PURPLE. Purple is a color for creative people. You like music and the arts. You enjoy visiting museums and taking pictures.

BLACK. Black is a mysterious color. You have secrets. You are very curious about many different things.

2 **Read the article again. Then circle the correct word to complete each sentence.**

1. People who like white are (honest)/ dishonest.

2. People who like yellow **like / don't like** trying new things.

3. People who like red are **good / bad** at making decisions.

4. People who like blue probably **like / don't like** trying new things.

5. People who like purple are usually **creative / boring**.

6. People who like black often **have / don't have** secrets.

The environment

A | Going green

1 Complete the text with one word from box A and one word from box B.

A	e-	global	hybrid	~~nuclear~~	organic	plastic	recycling	solar	wind
B	bags	bin	car	~~energy~~	energy	farm	food		warming	waste

Easy Ways You Can Help the Environment

1. Many people don't like __*nuclear energy*__ . They prefer to get their electricity from a _____ .

2. Buy and drive a _____ . They don't use as much gas as other cars, and they cause less pollution.

3. Take your own cloth bags to the supermarket. Don't use _____ .

4. Cook and eat _____ . It is safer for the environment.

5. Regular lightbulbs are not good for the environment. Use CFLs instead. This will help reduce _____ .

6. Put a large _____ in your house, and recycle paper, glass, and plastic.

7. When you buy a new computer, don't throw the old one away. If it still works, give it to a friend. This will help reduce _____ .

8. Use _____ to dry your clothes. Put your towels, blouses, shirts, pants, and even jeans on a clothesline to dry in the sun.

2 Write C (count noun) or N (noncount noun).

1. energy __N__
2. e-waste _____
3. lightbulb _____
4. recycling bin _____
5. pollution _____
6. plastic bag _____
7. bottle _____
8. landfill _____
9. plastic _____

3 Complete the sentences with *fewer* or *less*.

1. The world would be a better place with _____ less _____ e-waste.
2. People should use _____ plastic bags.
3. There should be _____ pollution in big cities.
4. There are _____ wind farms in the United States than in Europe.
5. Many people are trying to use _____ energy in their homes.
6. I'm sure you'll use _____ gas with your hybrid car.

4 Complete the letter with *too many* or *too much*.

LETTER TO THE EDITOR

June 17

I read the article *Building Goes Up Green* yesterday. It was very interesting, and I'm glad we're going to have a shopping mall that is better for the environment. There are _____ *too many* _____ buildings in this city that are bad for the environment. Most
                  1
buildings use _____ energy, so it's important that the new
                       2
buildings will use solar energy.

I think that the mall has a lot of creative ideas to help the environment in other ways, too. Using cloth bags is a wonderful idea. People will save money and help the environment at the same time. There are _____ plastic bags in
                                                      3
landfills around the world, and every little bit helps! I also think there are

_____ landfills in this city, so I'm glad the shopping mall plans to
        4
have a recycling center, too. People throw away _____ garbage,
                                                         5
and I hope this will help more people recycle.

I hope you write more articles about the mall.

Sincerely,

Dennis Armstrong

Environmental Student

5 Look at the web post. Then write sentences about what Mi-yon has. Use *not enough* or *too many*.

Thank you, friends! I almost have enough recycled things for my art project, but I still need a few more. If you have any of them, please send them to me at 556 Claremont Street.

	I needed	Now I have	I still need
1. plastic bottles	100	85	15
2. glass bottles	25	30	0
3. plastic bags	250	199	51
4. old lightbulbs	50	40	10
5. old toothbrushes	30	42	0
6. old CDs	175	170	5

Thanks!

Mi-yon Kam, Green Artist

1. *Mi-yon doesn't have enough plastic bottles.* _____
2. *She has too* _____ .
3. _____
4. _____
5. _____
6. _____

6 Answer the questions with your own information. Use quantifiers.

Example: *Yes, I do. I recycle paper. I could recycle more glass and plastic.* or
No, I don't, and I don't use enough cloth bags.

1. Do you recycle? _____
2. Do you have recycling bins in your home? _____
3. Does your town have enough recycling centers? _____
4. Do you use things in your home to save energy? _____
5. How much pollution is in your town? _____
6. How could you make less garbage in your home? _____

B *I'd rather not say.*

Complete each conversation with the expressions in the box.

> I'd say about   I'd rather not answer that

A. Larry: Hi, Kim. How's your new house?

Kim: It's great. We love the solar roof.

Larry: How much is your electric bill now?

Kim: *I'd* _____ $40 a month.
        ₁

Larry: Wow! That's cheap. How much did the solar roof cost?

Kim: _____ , but it was a
         ₂
good purchase. We save money each month, and we help the environment!

> I'd say maybe   I'd rather not say

B. Alice: Hi, Hala. Where are you going?

Hala: I'm going to the mall.

Alice: What are you going to buy?

Hala: Actually, _____ . It's a surprise for
          ₁
my sister's birthday.

Alice: Oh, OK. Well, I'll see you at her party. What time should I get there?

Hala: Oh, _____ around 6:00 p.m.
          ₂

Alice: OK.

> probably   I'd prefer not to say

C. Peng: Wow, Steve. I like your new car.

Steve: Thanks!

Peng: When did you get it?

Steve: Um, _____ about a month ago.
           ₁

Peng: Is it a hybrid car?

Steve: No, it isn't. The hybrid cars were too expensive.

Peng: Oh, that's too bad. How much do you spend on gas?

Steve: _____ , but definitely too much!
           ₂

C *What will happen?*

1 Circle the correct verb to complete each tip for helping the environment.

1. (Use)/ Grow / Take a clothesline.
2. Fix / Buy / Use leaky faucets.
3. Take / Pay / Buy local food.
4. Grow / Take / Pay public transportation.
5. Use / Pay / Fix rechargeable batteries.
6. Pay / Fix / Use cloth shopping bags.
7. Grow / Pay / Use your own food.
8. Take / Fix / Pay bills online.

2 Look at the pictures. Complete each sentence with the simple present of one tip from Exercise 1.

1. Debbie _uses a_ _____
   clothesline _____ .

2. Martin _____
   _____ .

3. Many people in big cities
   _____ .

  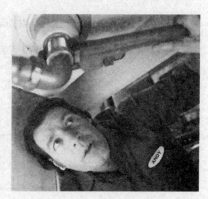

4. Wesley _____
   _____ .

5. Rita _____
   _____ .

6. Andy _____
   _____ .

3 Complete the story. Change the main clause of the last sentence to an *if* clause in the next sentence.

If I get a new car, I'll buy a hybrid car.

1. _If I buy a hybrid car_____ , I'll save money on gas.

2. _If I save_____ , I'll have more money to spend.

3. _____ , I'll buy a new cell phone.

4. _____ , I'll recycle my old cell phone.

5. _____ , there will be less e-waste.

6. _____ , the world will be a better place!

4 Write sentences with the phrases in the chart. Use the first conditional and *will*. Write each sentence two ways.

	Who	The condition	The result
1.	Robert	use rechargeable batteries	buy fewer batteries
2.	Emma	take public transportation	use less gas
3.	Tom and Jackie	have enough money	buy a hybrid car
4.	You	buy local food	get good fruit and vegetables
5.	We	recycle more bottles	help the environment

1. _If Robert uses rechargeable batteries, he'll buy fewer batteries._____

   _Robert will buy fewer batteries if he uses rechargeable batteries._____

2. _____

   _____

3. _____

   _____

4. _____

   _____

5. _____

   _____

5 Write the answers to the questions. Use the first conditional and the words in parentheses.

www.ecoblog.cup/Q&A

We want your opinions! Please tell us what you think!

What do you think will happen if more people recycle?

Marc67: *If more people recycle, we might have less garbage* .
1
(have less garbage / we / might)

SSGreen: *If more people* .
2
(could / help the environment / it)

What do you think will happen if our town starts a wind farm?

EcoJoe: _____ .
3
(use less energy / we / may)

EvaR22: _____ .
4
(be more jobs / might / there)

What do you think will happen if the big supermarket closes?

SSGreen: _____ .
5
(we / may / buy more local food)

EvaR22: _____ .
6
(some people / get upset / might)

6 Answer the questions with your own opinion. Use *will, may, might,* or *could*. Use each word at least once.

Example: *If people stop driving cars, there will be less pollution.* or

Many people might lose their jobs if people stop driving cars.

1. What will happen if people stop driving cars? _____

2. What will happen if everyone buys a bike? _____

3. What will happen if we don't have clean water? _____

4. What will happen if people don't fix leaky faucets? _____

5. What will happen if there is no more pollution? _____

6. What will happen if people have to pay for plastic bags in stores? _____

7. What will happen if you grow your own food? _____

8. What will happen if people buy new computers every year? _____

D Finding solutions

1 Read the article. Then check (✓) the chapters that might be in Chelsea Thomson's book.

1. ☐ How to Use Less Energy
2. ☐ How to Waste Time
3. ☐ How to Recycle More
4. ☐ Buy More Than You Need
5. ☐ How to Have More Garbage
6. ☐ How to Use Your Car Less Often
7. ☐ Where to Buy Local Food
8. ☐ Kinds of Food You Can Grow at Home

Dear Readers,

My new book, *Going Completely Green*, is finished! As the title says, I decided to go completely green for a month – no electricity, no running water, no car, no phone, no computer! I didn't even use anything with batteries. It was very difficult, and I decided to write a book about my experience. During the day, I wrote on paper with a pencil. When I wanted to sharpen my pencil, I remembered my pencil sharpener uses electricity. I had to sharpen it with a knife! At night, I used a candle for light. I washed all of my clothes by hand with water from the river behind my house, and then I put them on a clothesline. I walked to a local farm to buy food. I ate mostly fruits and vegetables. I only ate meat about five times, and I cooked it over a fire in my yard. The hardest part was not talking to friends and family on the phone or emailing them. My best friend lives an hour away by car, so I didn't communicate with her at all.

In my opinion, it is impossible to live completely green for a long time, but there are many things you can do. Now, I try to work with the lights off for most of the day. I'm driving my car again, but I try to walk or ride my bike when I only have to go a short distance. I buy more local food now, too. I have to use my computer for work, but I use it for fewer hours each day. I also turn it off when I'm not home. There are many things you can do to use less energy and water. This book will help you learn how to live a greener life. If you follow the steps in my book, you'll really help the environment. Oh, and if you buy my book, you might want to read it by candlelight to save energy!

Chelsea Thomson

2 Read the article again. Rewrite the sentences to correct the underlined mistakes.

1. Chelsea went green for <u>two months</u>.   *Chelsea went green for a month.*

2. She wrote <u>on a computer</u>.   _____

3. She washed her clothes <u>on a clothesline</u>.   _____

4. She thinks it's impossible <u>to work with the lights off</u>.   _____

5. Now she <u>drives her car</u> for short distances.   _____

6. She turns her computer off if <u>she's working</u>.   _____

Relationships

A Healthy relationships

1 Complete the sentences and the puzzle with the correct words. Use words about relationship behaviors.

Across

3. Mr. Jenkins said I didn't do a good job. He always finds things in my work to _____ .

6. Don and Greg _____ all the time. They never listen to each other.

7. Gina is really sorry. She's going to _____ to Kate.

8. Kate knows Gina is sorry. She's going to _____ her.

Down

1. My mother likes to _____ my friends. She always tells me if they are good or bad friends.

2. Please don't _____ . I know you're not being honest.

3. Josh and Dan usually _____ by email, but they sometimes talk on the phone.

4. I want to go to a restaurant, and you want to go to the park. Let's _____ and eat food in the park!

5. Shannon talks about everyone! I hate when people _____ .

2 Complete the advice column. Use the infinitive forms of the correct verbs from the box.

apologize	argue	be	communicate	compromise	✓lie

Ask Lee

Dear Lee,

Sometimes it's difficult to tell my parents the truth. I'm a pretty good son, but I make mistakes. I don't want my parents to get upset. I know that it's not good
<u>to lie</u> , but sometimes
   1
it's hard to be honest. What's your advice?

          – Stressed-Out Son

Dear Stressed-Out Son,
It's not always easy

_____ honest, but you
   2
should try. It's very important

_____ with your
   3
parents. If you say you made a mistake, it might help them understand. They used to be young, and they made mistakes, too.

Dear Lee,
My friends and I are planning a vacation, and we're arguing. Two people want to go to the beach, and one person wants to go hiking. What should we do?

          – Ralph

Dear Ralph,
It's never a good idea

_____ with your
   4
friends. It's important

_____ . Why don't
   5
you go to a park with mountains near the ocean, like the Manuel Antonio National Park in Costa Rica? You can hike in the mountains and go to the beach!

Dear Lee,
I gossiped about my friend to some other people. I feel terrible, and now she won't talk to me. Please help!

          – Pamela G.

Dear Pamela,
When someone is upset with you, it's

useful _____ . If she
   6
doesn't want to talk to you, tell her you're sorry in an email. If she knows how you feel, she may forgive you.

3 Put the words in the correct order to make a sentence.

1. It's / to help / your neighbors / a good idea / .

   It's a good idea to help your neighbors.

2. to apologize / It's / nice / when you're wrong / .

   _____

3. with your teacher / not good / It's / to argue / .

   _____

4. It's / to compromise / important / with your friends / .

   _____

5. helpful / It's / in class / to listen carefully / .

   _____

6. never a good idea / about your friends / It's / to gossip / .

   _____

4 Complete the sentences with your own ideas. Use expressions from the box.

It's (not) a good idea	It's (not) helpful	It's (not) useful
It's (not) good	It's (not) important	

Example: At school: *It's important to be on time.*

At school:

1. _____ (be) on time.

2. _____ (use) a dictionary in class.

With your friends:

3. _____ (communicate) dishonestly

   or impatiently.

4. _____ (plan) activities that

   everyone enjoys.

At a library:

5. _____ (talk) quietly.

6. _____ (write) in the books.

I'm really sorry.

1 Circle the correct phrase to complete each conversation.

A.

Kelly: Hi, Doug. **That's OK** / (**I'm really sorry**)
I missed your birthday.
   1

Doug: **There's no need to apologize.** / **I'm sorry.**
               2

Kelly: Well, it's not nice to miss a friend's birthday.

Doug: Please, Kelly. **I'm sorry.** / **Don't worry about it.**
                                    3

Kelly: OK. But let's celebrate on Friday.

Doug: Great!

B. **Kelly:** Hi, Doug. **There's no need to**
apologize / **I'm sorry,** but I can't
        1
make it on Friday.

Doug: **That's OK.** / **My apologies.**
                2

Kelly: No, it's not. I feel terrible.

My apologies. / **Don't worry about**
                   3
it. Can you come over on Saturday?
I'll make dinner!

Doug: OK. That sounds great.

2 Complete the conversations. Use some of the expressions from Exercise 1
and your own ideas.

A. **You:** I missed your party. _____ .
                                                    1

Friend: Oh, _____ . What happened?
                              2

You: _____ .
                        3

Friend: That's too bad.

B. **Friend:** I am very late. _____ .
                                            1

You: _____ . Is everything all right?
                        2

Friend: Not really. _____ .
                                3

You: Oh. Too bad!

C *That can't be the problem.*

1 Complete each question with the correct word from the box.

✓after	into	together
along	on	up
by	on	up

1. Do you take _____ **after** _____ anyone in your family? Who?

2. Have you ever been picked _____ in school? By whom?

3. Do you get _____ well with your friends?

4. Have you ever broken _____ with a fiancé or fiancée? Who?

5. How often do you get _____ with friends each month? What do you do?

6. Do you like it when friends drop _____ and don't call first? Who does this?

7. Who is the last person you ran _____ when you were shopping?

8. Do you know anyone who is immature and needs to grow _____ ? Who?

9. Who is the person you count _____ the most?

2 Answer the questions in Exercise 1 with your own information. Use phrasal verbs, and add more information when possible.

Example: _Yes, I do. I take after my mother. We're friendly and outgoing. I look_
like her, too. or

No, I don't. But I'd like to take after my father. He's really intelligent.

1. _____

2. _____

3. _____

4. _____

5. _____

6. _____

7. _____

8. _____

9. _____

3 Complete the sentences with the correct words from the box.

can't	may	✓must

1. Cindy _____**must**_____ get along well with her family. She's at her parents' house every weekend.

2. I'm not sure, but I think I _____ know where the restaurant is.

3. Mark _____ be breaking up with me! He loves me!

could	might not	must not

4. Bev _____ come to work today. She felt sick yesterday.

5. Josh _____ be coming to the party. It started an hour ago, and he's not here.

6. You _____ run into Dan at the mall. I think he's shopping today.

4 Complete the conversation with *must, can't,* or *might.*

Sandra: Good morning, Paul. Do you know where Dan is? I didn't see his car outside.

Paul: I'm not sure. He _____**might**_____ be at a
1
doctor's appointment.

Sandra: No, he _____ have a doctor's
2
appointment today. I have all his appointments in my calendar.

Paul: You're right. He _____ be taking
3
the bus today. The buses are often late.

Sandra: Well, he _____ have a good reason. He's never late.
4

Paul: Wait! My phone's ringing. It _____ be Dan. Let me see. . . .
5
No. It _____ be Dan. It's not his number.
6

Sandra: Well, you should answer it! Dan _____ be calling from a different
7
phone if there's a problem.

A minute later . . .

Paul: Yes. It was Dan. He _____ be feeling pretty stressed. He ran out
8
of gas and had to ask a stranger to drive him to a gas station. But he left his cell
phone in his car, so he had to ask the stranger to use her phone.

5 Answer the questions with your own ideas. Use words from the box to speculate and to say how sure you are.

can't	could	may (not)	might (not)	must (not)

Example: *I don't know. She might be looking for some money.* or

I see her car. She must be looking for her keys.

1. What is the woman looking for?

_____

2. What animal is it?

_____

3. Why is the boy crying?

_____

4. Why are they arguing?

_____

5. Why is the woman late?

_____

6. Where are they going?

_____

1 Read the advice. Who is the speaker giving the advice to? Write the correct heading from the magazine article.

1. "I'm sorry, but you need to get more organized.   <u>To a co-worker</u>
   Your work is often late."

2. "It must feel bad that James doesn't want to play   _____
   with you. Could you ask Kahil?"

3. "I don't think he's good for you. Do you ever think   _____
   about breaking up?"

How to Give Advice

Everyone has an opinion, but sometimes it's not easy to give advice. This is really true for important relationships. Here are some tips on how you can give advice in different relationships.

To a child If you aren't careful, children might get angry when you give them advice. They are often immature, and they don't understand that you want to help. It's useful to tell them you understand what they are going through before you give them advice. Be considerate, think about how they might feel, and remember that their opinions matter. It's not helpful to speak loudly or to criticize; this makes children feel worse, and they might not listen to you.

To a co-worker It can be difficult to give advice to people at work, so it's often good to apologize first. For example, say, "I'm sorry, but I think you could . . ." And remember that it's never a good idea to judge people. Give advice about what you think should change about the person's work, not about the person! Also remember that in work

situations, you often have to compromise. You may give advice, but the person might not take it!

To a friend Friends can be the hardest people to give advice to. It's important to be honest, but you should also be kind. When you give advice to a friend, don't argue. Try to communicate with your friend. Ask questions and really understand your friend's problem before you give advice.

These tips are useful in other types of relationships, too. The important thing to remember is to be patient with others, and give them a chance to respond to your advice. It's also helpful to give advice when the person is ready to listen. Don't give advice when the person is extremely upset or stressed. Try to find a time when he or she is more relaxed.

2 Read the article again. Check (✓) what the writer says about giving advice.

1. Don't argue.   ☑   4. Be honest.   ☐

2. You may need to compromise.   ☐   5. Don't give advice about work.   ☐

3. You might need to get angry.   ☐   6. Ask questions.   ☐

Living your life

A *He taught himself.*

1 Complete the puzzle with words for qualities for success. What's the mystery word?

1. a strong interest in something

2. the quality of showing no fear

3. the ability to change easily

4. a commitment to something

5. the belief that you can succeed

6. the ability to develop original ideas

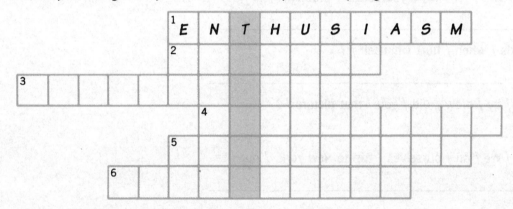

1. | E | N | T | H | U | S | I | A | S | M |

2 Circle the correct words to complete the article.

Man Saves Friend

Farmers Jim Rolland and Ryan Jensen were trying to take soybeans out of a large bin, but they wouldn't come out. Jim Rolland was **confident** / **confidence** that he could fix the problem, but his **confident** / **confidence** got him in trouble. He climbed some stairs and went into the bin. The beans moved and covered him completely!

Ryan Jensen told another worker to call for help. Then he had a **creative** / **creativity** idea. He wasn't sure it was **wise** / **wisdom**, but he also went into the bin. He got on his stomach on top of the beans. For four hours, he moved beans so Rolland could breathe. His **dedicated** / **dedication** and **brave** / **bravery** saved his friend's life.

Rescue workers finally came. They removed the beans and helped Rolland out of the bin. He was fine, and he was happy to have **talented** / **talent** people help him.

3 Put the words in the correct order to make sentences.

1. a picture of / art class / myself / I / painted / in / .

   I painted a picture of myself in art class.

2. by / The / isn't / itself / computer / going to work / .

   _____

3. brave / herself / doesn't / mother / My / consider / .

   _____

4. Japanese / themselves / taught / Kyle / and Mick / .

   _____

5. blame / Don't / for / my / yourselves / problems / !

   _____

6. did / Chris / When / hurt / himself / ?

   _____

7. yourself / by / draw / Did / you / that picture / ?

   _____

8. enjoyed / We / on / ourselves / trip to New York / our / .

   _____

4 Complete the sentences with the correct reflexive pronouns.

What do people like to do by _____themselves_____ ? Here's what some
                                      1
of our readers said:

- I like to travel by _____ . I always meet interesting people,
                              2
  and sometimes they teach me words of wisdom. (Tom P., Chicago)

- My brother and I love to play video games by _____ .
                                                        3
  We don't like our sisters to play with us. (Jake M., San Antonio)

- My husband likes to cook by _____ . And that's OK with
                                       4
  me! (Lidia S., Boston)

- My daughter is very enthusiastic, and she likes to do extreme sports by

  _____ . It makes me nervous! (Na-young K., San Francisco)
         5

What do you like to do by _____ ?
                                   6

5 Complete the conversations with the correct personal and reflexive pronouns.

A. **Rachel:** _____I_____ like your scarf, Phoebe.
   1

   Phoebe: Thanks. I made it by _____ .
   2

   Rachel: Wow. _____ have a lot of talent!
   3

B. **Sheila:** Look! My son painted this by _____ .
   1

   Feng: _____ did a great job.
   2

C. **Joe:** Did you hear what happened to Emily?

   Martin: No, _____ didn't.
   1

   Joe: She hurt _____ skiing.
   2

   Martin: Is _____ OK?
   3

   Joe: Yes, she is.

D. **Laura:** We really enjoyed _____ at your party, Pedro.
   1

   Pedro: I'm glad _____ had fun, but the food I made was terrible.
   2

   Laura: Don't blame _____ . It was fine.
   3

   Pedro: You're right. My friends enjoyed _____ . That's what counts!
   4

6 Answer the questions with your own information.

Example: <u>*Yes, I do. I'm very enthusiastic about good music.*</u> or

   <u>*No, I don't. I'm not enthusiastic about anything.*</u>

1. Do you consider yourself enthusiastic? What are you enthusiastic about? _____

   _____

2. Do you consider yourself flexible, or do you like to do things your own way? _____

   _____

3. What do you like to do by yourself? _____

   _____

4. Have you ever painted yourself? What did the picture look like? _____

   _____

5. Do you know someone who hurt himself or herself playing a sport? What happened? _____

   _____

6. Do you think people should travel by themselves? Why or why not? _____

   _____

I'll give it some thought.

1 Write the conversation in the correct order.

2
> Their prices are really high. You should go to Comp.com. It's an online store.
> ✓ Hi, Tina. Where are you going?
> Hmm. . . . I'll give it some thought. Thanks.
> I don't think you should do that.
> I'm going to Tech-It to buy a new computer.
> Really? Why not?

Erin: _Hi, Tina. Where are you going?_ _____

Tina: _____

Erin: _____

Tina: _____

Erin: _____

Tina: _____

2 Complete the conversations. Use information from the pictures and sentences from the box. Use Exercise 1 as a model. Sometimes more than one answer is possible.

> I wouldn't recommend that.   I'll think about it.
> I'll see.   I'm not sure that's the best idea.

1. **Ed:** Hi, Ali. Where are you going?

   Ali: I'm going to _____ to

   buy a new _____ .

   Ed: _____ .

   Ali: Really? _____ ?

   Ed: Their prices are really high. You should go

   to _____ . It's an

   _____ store.

   Ali: Hmm. . . . _____ .

   Thanks.

2. **Sasha:** Hi, Marc. _____ ?

   Marc: I'm going to _____

   _____ .

   Sasha: _____ .

   Marc: Really? _____ ?

   Sasha: Their prices are really high.

   _____

   _____ ,

   Marc: Hmm. . . . _____ .

   Thanks.

C What would you do?

1 Rewrite the sentences. Change the underlined words. Use the phrasal verb in parentheses and the correct pronoun.

1. Can you <u>show me where Linda is</u>? (point out)

   Can you point her out?

2. You need to <u>do your homework again</u>. It has a lot of mistakes. (do over)

   _____

3. I <u>didn't accept that job</u>. (turn down)

   _____

4. I'm going to <u>donate these shirts</u>. (give away)

   _____

5. Please don't <u>mention his daughter</u>. (bring up)

   _____

6. When are you going to <u>return the money I lent you</u>? (pay back)

   _____

7. We really should <u>discuss our problem</u>. (talk over)

   _____

8. Can I <u>use this computer</u> before I buy it? (try out)

   _____

9. I'll <u>return your camera</u> tomorrow, if that's OK. (give back)

   _____

10. Let's <u>do the conference call later</u>. (put off)

   _____

2 Complete Bianca's email with the correct forms of the verbs in parentheses. Use the second conditional.

To: RobbieJ@cup.org
From: Bianca54@cup.com
Subject: What would you do?

Hi Rob,

I have some interesting news. My aunt might give me some money! I _**would do**___
                                                                              1
(do) so many things if I _____ (have) a lot of money. If I
                                      2
_____ (be) rich, I _____ (not work) anymore! That
          3   4
would be great. If I _____ (not have) a job, I _____
                              5   6
(travel) around the world. I _____ (feel) very lucky if I
                                        7
_____ (get) a lot of money. What would you do?
          8
Your friend,

Bianca

3 Now complete Rob's email with the correct forms of the verbs in parentheses. Use the second conditional.

To: Bianca54@cup.com
From: RobbieJ@cup.org
Subject: RE: What would you do?

Hey Bianca!

Wow! It _**would be**_____ (be) great if your aunt _____ (give)
                  1   2
you money. Is it a lot of money? If I _____ (have) a lot of money, I
                                                3
_____ (make) a big, beautiful garden. But I can't have a garden at my
          4
apartment, so I _____ (need) a house with a big yard. I
                              5
_____ (use) a lot of my money to buy a house, and there
          6
_____ (be) a lot of room for two big gardens: a vegetable garden and a
          7
flower garden. I _____ (give) some money to my brother, too, if I
                              8
_____ (be) rich. He _____ (not have to pay) me back.
          9   10
Take care,

Rob

4 Write questions with the words in parentheses. Use the second conditional.

1. (What / you / do / if / you / be / braver)

   What would you do if you were braver?
   _____

2. (What / you / buy / for your friends / if / you / have / a lot of money)

   _____

3. (Where / you / go / if / you / have / a free ticket)

   _____

4. (What / you / do / if / you / have / 200 vacation days)

   _____

5. (What instrument / you / play / if / you and your friends / have / a band)

   _____

6. (What sport / you / try / if / you / try / an extreme sport)

   _____

7. (What / you / give away / if / you / move)

   _____

5 Answer the questions in Exercise 4 with your own information.

Example: *If I were braver, I would take a trip around the world by myself.*

1. _____
2. _____
3. _____
4. _____
5. _____
6. _____
7. _____

D What an accomplishment!

1 Read the letter. Then circle the correct answers.

1. How old is Thomas?   99   100   101

2. Who is Peter?   his brother   his son   his grandson

Dear Peter,

Can you believe I'll be 100 years old next week? If I had a dollar for every great thing I did, I would be rich! I decided to write to you about a few important things that happened in each decade of my life.

1920s – These are the first years I really remember. Pop music was extremely popular, and I was in a pop band. We were very dedicated to our music!

1930s – Many people didn't have a lot of money in the 1930s, but I worked very hard. In 1937, I bought myself a car! If I had that car today, it would be worth a lot of money!

1940s – This was a sad decade because of World War II, but the 1940s were also happy for me in many ways. I met your grandmother in 1941 when I was a soldier. A friend pointed her out to me at the supermarket. We got married two years later. That was a wise decision! Your mother was born in 1944.

1950s – We bought our first TV. I remember trying it out in the store first. It was amazing! And with the Civil Rights Movement starting, it was a good time to have a TV.

1960s – This was a very creative time in my life. Your grandmother was painting, and I started taking pictures. In 1969, a man walked on the moon!

1970s – I was offered a promotion in 1972, but I turned it down. I retired six years later.

1980s – I started a volunteer program at a hospital in 1982 and was busy with that for several years.

1990s – In 1995, a park in our town was dedicated to me for the volunteer work I did at the hospital. Do you remember when you bought me a computer in 1997? I never taught myself how to use it!

2000s – The 2000s were a quiet decade, but I've had a lot of time to spend with family. I bought a cell phone this year, but I took it back. I didn't think I really needed it. I guess I'm a little old-fashioned!

See you next week for my birthday!

Your grandfather,

Thomas O'Malley

---

2 Read the letter again. Then number the events in the correct order.

_____ He turned down a promotion.		_____ He got a cell phone.
_____ He got married.		_____ He bought a car.
_____ He started a volunteer program.		_____ He started taking pictures.
_1_ He was in a pop band.		_____ He got a computer.

Music

A Music trivia

1 Put the words in the correct order to make phrases about music. Add hyphens, if necessary.

1. best / artist / selling   _best-selling artist_
2. video / winning / award   _____
3. performer / often / downloaded   _____
4. priced / high / ticket   _____
5. group / named / oddly   _____
6. singers / well / known   _____
7. breaking / hit / record   _____
8. nice / voice / sounding   _____

2 Complete the webpage with the phrases from Exercise 1.

Jake and Jill's Music Awards

Hello fans! Here's today's music news from your favorite music fans!

- Sting, a _best-selling artist_ from the 1980s, and his wife started the Rainforest Concert in 1991. They have the concert every two years. This year, _____, like Elton John and Bruce Springsteen, performed. Tickets were $2,500 or more! That's a _____, but all of the money helps save rain forests around the world.

- Listen to *Yellow Fever!* It's a great album by Señor Coconut and His Orchestra. Yes, this is a very _____ (*señor* is a Spanish word, but Señor Coconut is actually German), but we think each singer has a very _____!

- Who is the most _____ on our website? Taylor Swift! Her song "Love Story" has been downloaded over 4 million times, and the video won the Country Music Association Award for Best Music Video in 2009. To listen to her _____, *click here*. To watch her _____, *click here*.

3 Complete the sentences with the correct forms of the words in parentheses. Use the past passive.

We Are the World

Kenny Rogers and Lionel Richie

"We Are the World" _**was recorded**_ (record) in 1985.
___(1)___

The money it made _____ (give) to groups
___(2)___

that help hungry people in Africa. The song

_____ (write) by Michael and Lionel
___(3)___

Richie. Many famous singers, like Kenny, Bob, and

Stevie, _____ (ask) to sing it.
___(4)___

A video _____ (make) while the singers were recording the song. The song
___(5)___

and video _____ (play) on TV in the spring of 1985.
___(6)___

In 2010, "We Are the World" _____ (record) again with new singers to help
___(7)___

the people of Haiti. The song _____ (sing) by over 80 well-known musicians,
___(8)___

like Bieber and Hudson. It _____ (see) on TV by many people
___(9)___

on February 12.

4 Rewrite each sentence in the past passive. If there is information about who did the action, use a *by* phrase.

1. Four men planned the Woodstock Festival in 1969.

   **The Woodstock Festival was planned by four men in 1969.**

2. Someone asked many well-known singers to sing at Woodstock.

   _____

3. Someone gave information about the festival on the radio.

   _____

4. Someone allowed about 400,000 to 500,000 music fans into the festival.

   _____

5. People made a documentary about Woodstock in 1970.

   _____

5 Look at the chart of some record-breaking hits. Then answer the questions. Use the past passive.

Song	Singer(s)	Year of release	Millions of recordings sold
Candle in the Wind		1997	37
White Christmas		1942	30
We Are the World		1985	20
Around the Clock		1954	17
Hey Jude		1968	10
It's Now or Never		1960	10

1. When was "White Christmas" released? _____

2. When was "Hey Jude" sung by? _____

3. How many recordings of "We Are the World" were sold? _____

4. What song was released in 1954? _____

5. What song was sung in 1997? _____

6. When was "Hey Jude" released? _____

6 Answer the questions with your own information. Write complete sentences.

Example: __My favorite song was "Candle in the Wind."__

1. What was your favorite song when you were 12? _____

2. Who was it sung by? _____

3. What kind of music was it? _____

4. Was a video made of the song? What was it like? _____

5. Was the singer or group well known? _____

6. Is the singer or group well known today? _____

7. Did you ever go to a concert of the singer or group? Where was it? _____

8. Was a documentary ever made about the singer or group? What was it called? _____

B *The first thing you do is . . .*

Rewrite the instructions. Use the words in the box.

A.

> **How to Buy a Song**
> 1. Find the song you want, and click on it.
> 2. Enter your credit card number.
> 3. Read the information, and click "Yes."

| After that | ✓ First | To finish |

How to Buy a Song

First, find the song you want, and click on it.

_____

_____

B.

> **How to Listen to Music on Your Phone**
> 1. Open your music program.
> 2. Choose the song you want to listen to.
> 3. Click "Play."

| The last thing you do is | Then | To start |

How to Listen to Music on Your Phone

_____

_____

C.

> **How to Record Your Voice**
> 1. Put the recorder near you.
> 2. Hit the "Record" button.
> 3. Sing a song or speak into the recorder.

| Finally | Next | The first thing you do is |

How to Record Your Voice

_____

_____

_____

C Music and me

1 Complete the sentences and the puzzle with the correct verbs.

Across

1. My favorite band will _____ a new album next week.

5. Justin sang the song "My World," but he didn't _____ it.
   Mark was one of the producers.

7. Coldplay will _____ their tour dates on their website.

8. Beethoven couldn't hear anything, but he was able to _____ great music.
   Many people listen to his music today, almost 200 years after he died.

Down

2. He likes to _____ his audience in his concerts.

3. I can't sing very well, but I really _____ music. I listen to it all the time.

4. Do you know when your brother's band is going to _____ their new song?
   I really would like to go see his band.

6. We're going to _____ our new song in the studio next week.
   They have new computers we can use.

2 Circle the correct word to complete each sentence.

1. Beethoven's Fifth Symphony is my favorite musical **compose / (composition)**.

2. My favorite band **released / a release** a new album yesterday.

3. My uncle **produces / production** songs, but he can't sing or play an instrument.

4. Jonathan found one of his father's old **record / recordings**.

5. Mike loves to go to **perform / performances** at music festivals.

6. My sister likes to **entertain / entertainment** our family.

7. The band made an **announce / announcement** about their tour yesterday.

8. What time does the **produce / production** of *Hamlet* start?

3 Answer the questions with your own information. Write complete sentences.

Example: *My favorite kind of entertainment is the movies.*

1. What's your favorite kind of entertainment?_____

2. Have you ever taken a music class? When? _____

3. Have you ever heard your favorite singer perform? Where? _____

4. Have you ever been to a party for an album release? Where? _____

5. What kind of music do you appreciate? _____

4 Complete the email with *yet* or *already*.

To: Lee1988@cup.org
From: JJJ@cup.com
Subject: Do you have plans on Friday night?

Hey Lee!

Have you made plans for Friday night _____*yet*_____ ? My brother's band,
                                                          1
Time Travel, is playing at the Music Café. I've _____ seen them
                                                                              2
about ten times, and they're great! Have you listened to the CD I sent you

_____ ? I've _____ bought tickets for my sister
           3   4
and me, but I haven't gotten a ticket for you _____ . Let me know
                                                                   5
if you want to go. Tickets aren't high-priced. They're only $10. Time Travel has

_____ started recording their next CD. It hasn't been released
           6
_____ , but they might play a few songs from it on Friday. I hope
           7
you can come!

Jay

5 Look at Carla's To-Do list. Then write sentences about what she has and hasn't done. Use the present perfect with *yet* or *already*.

> <u>To Do</u>
> ○ Send Jen and Sandra information about the Coldplay concert ✔
> ○ Call Sandra and Jen about tickets to see Coldplay ✔
> Buy the tickets ✔
> ○ Clean the house
> Go to the airport to pick up Jen and Sandra

1. <u>*Carla has already sent Jen and Sandra information about the Coldplay concert.*</u>
2. <u>*She*</u> _____
3. _____
4. _____
5. _____

6 Look at Jen and Sandra's To-Do list. Then write questions and answers about what they have and haven't done. Use the present perfect with *yet* or *already*.

> <u>To Do</u>
> ○ Do the laundry ✔
> ○ Clean the apartment ✔
> Listen to Coldplay's new songs
> ○ Give our parents Carla's cell phone number ✔
> Pay Carla for the tickets

1. Question: <u>*Have Jen and Sandra done the laundry yet?*</u>

   Answer: <u>*Yes, they have already done the laundry.*</u>
2. Q: <u>*Have they*</u> _____

   A: _____
3. Q: _____

   A: _____
4. Q: _____

   A: _____
5. Q: _____

   A: _____

D | Thoughts on music

1 Read the article. Then write why musicians don't want people to give music to their friends.

_____

Music Laws

Today, many people get their music from the Internet. But is it legal? It depends on how you get the music and what country you live in. It's sometimes OK, but it's often against the law.

It is usually legal to buy songs from websites on the Internet. If you buy a song, you can make a copy for yourself. However, in the United States and some other countries, it is illegal to make copies of the song for your friends. This is because laws protect people's ideas and work. If everyone copied and gave music to their friends, people would not buy the singers' albums, and musicians couldn't make money for their work.

Also, in many countries it's illegal to *bootleg* music. This is a word that describes when people go to a live performance, record the music, and then upload the music to the Internet to give to their friends or to sell. Sometimes at concerts musicians perform new songs before they are recorded in a studio. They don't want their music released on the Internet before their albums are sold.

Some people *sample* music when they compose songs. This means they use a part of someone else's song in their music. This is often done in pop music. Sampling is usually legal if you have permission from the singer, but it is usually not OK to use someone else's music without permission.

Interesting Music Trivia

• In 1990, part of a David Bowie song was sampled by Vanilla Ice without permission. After the song was released, Vanilla Ice had to pay David Bowie a lot of money for using his music.

• In 1999, Napster was created as a way to get music from friends without paying for it on the Internet. Napster had to stop doing this in the United States, and now people have to pay for the music.

2 Read the article. Then write L (legal – OK) or I (illegal – not OK) for these actions according to the laws in the United States.

1. You can buy songs on the Internet from websites. __*L*__

2. You can get a song for free from a friend. _____

3. You can bootleg music from a live performance. _____

4. You can sample music without permission. _____

On vacation

A Travel preferences

1 Complete the travel ads with the correct phrases from the box.

buy handicrafts	listen to live music	✓speak a foreign language	visit landmarks
	see wildlife	try local food	volunteer

European Vacation

Can you ___speak a___
___foreign language___ ?
  1
If you speak French,
Spanish, or Portuguese, this
is the vacation for you! Visit
France, Spain, and Portugal.
_____ ,
                2
like the Eiffel Tower in France and famous
museums in Spain, or stay near the ocean
in Portugal.

South American Working Vacation

Visit Peru and Ecuador in a different way.
_____ your time to
                 3
help people and animals. First, teach English
in Peru, and then work in the Amazon rain
forest. You'll _____ ,
                        4
like frogs, river dolphins, and monkeys.

Miami Dream

The weather is wonderful in
Miami for most of the year.
Visit beaches during the day.
At night, There are also
many places to
_____ .
          5
You can go to a concert or listen to
in the parks or even on the beach.

Seoul Markets

Do you like shopping? Tour Seoul's markets.
Namdaemun is the largest market in Seoul, and
it sells many different things. You can
_____ , like bags and
          6
jewelry. You can even _____
                                7
while you are shopping at the market or take
some home to cook.

2 Put the words in the correct order to make sentences. Make one of the words a gerund. Use the simple present forms of the other verbs.

1. be / by boat / Travel / very slow

   Traveling by boat is very slow.

2. enjoy / I / foreign languages / speak / when I travel

   _____

3. buy / handicrafts for my cousins / I / in local markets / like

   _____

4. be / to cook / I / interested in / learn / Thai food

   _____

5. be / to do on vacation / landmarks / my favorite thing / Visit

   _____

6. be / concerned about / help / I / wildlife in the ocean

   _____

3 Complete the conversation with the gerund forms of the correct words from the box.

go	✓hike	travel	volunteer	volunteer

Mark: Hey, Jesse. Where are you going for vacation?

Jesse: I don't know. I enjoy _____*hiking*_____ in
$\qquad\qquad\quad$₁
the mountains. Any suggestions?

Mark: How about the Rockies in Canada?

Jesse: I don't think so. I prefer _____
$\qquad\qquad\qquad\qquad\quad$2
somewhere warm.

Mark: Why don't you go to Costa Rica? There are
mountains there, and it's warm.

Jesse: That's a good idea. You know, I'm interested in _____ .
$\qquad\qquad\qquad\qquad\qquad\qquad\qquad\qquad\qquad$3
Maybe I could help animals there.

Mark: _____ is a great idea. It should make the vacation cheaper,
$\qquad\quad$4
too. Are you going by yourself?

Jesse: No, I'm not. I dislike _____ alone. I'm going with friends.
$\qquad\qquad\qquad\qquad\qquad$5

90 Unit 12 Lesson A

4 Look at the chart. Then complete the sentences.

Name	Travel activity	Opinion	Preference
Cara	travel / by bus	slow	go / by train
Diego	drive / a car	dangerous	ride / a bike
Donna and Nicole	visit / landmarks	boring	see / wildlife
Tom	go / to clubs	not fun	go / to concerts
Ian and Meg	travel / by plane	expensive	stay / home
Libby	learn / Chinese	difficult	study / Spanish

1. Cara thinks _traveling by bus is slow_ . She prefers _going by train_ .

2. Diego thinks _____ . He _____ .

3. Donna and Nicole think _____ . They _____ .

4. Tom thinks _____ . He _____ .

5. Ian and Meg _____ . They _____ .

6. Libby _____ . She _____ .

5 Answer the questions with your own information. Use gerunds when possible.

Example: _I'm interested in buying handicrafts and trying local food._

1. What vacation activities are you interested in? _____

2. What do you enjoy doing on vacation? _____

3. What do you dislike doing on vacation? _____

4. What do you think is the easiest way to travel? _____

5. What do you think is the cheapest way to travel? _____

6. What do you dislike about planning a vacation? _____

7. What are you concerned about when looking for a hotel? _____
   _____

8. What do you worry about when you travel? _____

9. Do you like listening to live local music when you travel? What kind? _____
   _____

10. Are you interested in writing about your vacations? Why or why not? _____
    _____

B Don't forget to . . .

Complete the conversations with sentences from the box.

> Don't forget to get to the station 20 minutes early.
> Let me remind you to get there before 8:00 p.m.
> Remember to look for plane tickets today.
> ✓Would you like a bus ticket or a train ticket?
> Would you prefer one bed or two beds?
> Would you rather go to a warm place or a cold place?

A. Mr. Harris: Hello. Can I help you?

    Richard: Yes. I'd like a ticket for Chicago, please.

    Mr. Harris: OK. _Would you like a bus ticket_
                          1
                   or a train ticket ?
                       1

    Richard: Oh, well, which one is better?

    Mr. Harris: The bus takes longer, but it's cheaper.

    Richard: Hmm. . . . I'll take the bus. I'm going on Saturday morning.

    Mr. Harris: Good. A bus leaves at 9:15. _____ .
                                        2

    Richard: OK. Thanks.

B.   **Blanca:** Hey, Erica. _____ .
                                1

    Erica: Oh, yeah. Thanks. I'll look for the best tickets online after work.

    _____ ?
                        2

    Blanca: Let's go somewhere hot, like the beach.

    Erica: OK. I'll look for some cheap tickets, and we can make plans tonight.

    Blanca: Great. Thanks.

C.   **Ms. Ito:** Can I help you?

    Shan: Yes, I need a room for three nights.

    Ms. Ito: No problem. _____ ?
                             1

    Shan: One bed, please. Oh, and is there a restaurant in this hotel?

    Ms. Ito: Yes, there is. It's right over there. _____ .
                                                2
    It closes at 8:30.

Rules and recommendations

1 Complete the words for the extreme sports.

1. p*aragliding*
2. r_____
   c_____
3. b_____
   j_____
4. w_____
   w_____
   r_____
5. k_____
   s_____
6. w_____
7. s_____
8. s_____

2 Circle the correct expression to complete each sentence.

1. **Necessity:** _____ fill out this form before you go paragliding.

   a. You don't have to   (b.) You must   c. You'd better

2. **Recommendation:** Sandra _____ plan her vacation before she goes.

   a. doesn't have to   b. must   c. ought to

3. **Lack of necessity:** You _____ wear warm clothes when rock climbing in the summer.

   a. don't have to   b. have to   c. shouldn't

4. **Necessity:** Nancy and Carol _____ wear heavy boots when they go snowboarding.

   a. should   b. shouldn't   c. have to

5. **Recommendation:** _____ take sunglasses when you go white-water rafting.

   a. You must   b. You've got to   c. You'd better

6. **Lack of necessity:** Jorge _____ go skydiving if he doesn't want to.

   a. has to   b. doesn't have to   c. shouldn't

7. **Necessity:** _____ pay for my kite surfing lessons before I can take the first lesson.

   a. I've got to   b. I don't have to   c. I'd better

8. **Recommendation:** Sue and Teddy _____ go bungee jumping. It's very dangerous.

   a. don't have to   b. have got to   c. shouldn't

3 Complete the article with *must* or *should*.

✈ How to Get to Your Flight Faster

Airports have a lot of rules. Here are some tips to help you get through the airport faster.

Airport Security

- You ___*should*___ print your boarding pass at home,

1
  if possible.

- You _____ get to the airport early. It's a good

2
  idea to arrive an hour before your flight.

- You _____ have your passport or other ID.

3
  You can't get on the plane without one of them.

- You _____ take off your shoes at security.

4
  They won't let you go through with them on.

- You _____ wear shoes that are easy to take off.

5
  You'll move faster.

4 Circle the correct words to complete the instructions.

Welcome to the Riverside Park white-water rafting trip. We want you to have a safe trip, so there are a few things that you **(have to)** / **don't have to** do.
¹
First of all, **you'd better** / **you shouldn't** listen to your guide. That's me, so please
²
listen to me carefully. Now for the safety rules: **You must not** / **You must** sit on the
³
raft at all times. Stand only when you are getting on or off the raft. And while we are
riding, you **don't have to** / **ought to** hold on to the raft.
⁴

It's going to be warm today, so you **don't have to** / **must** wear a coat, but you
⁵
should / **shouldn't** wear a hat. It will protect your skin and eyes from the sun. Later
⁶
we'll stop at a beach and have lunch there. **You shouldn't** / **You'd better** eat on the raft.
⁷
Finally, don't forget that rafting can be dangerous. **You don't have to** / **You've got to**
⁸
be careful all day. If you follow my instructions, you'll be safe and have fun!

5 Write your own rules and recommendations for each place. Use modals for necessity, lack of necessity, and recommendations.

Example: **In a restaurant:** 1. *You must pay for your food.*

2. *You don't have to eat something you don't like.*

3. *You should leave a little extra money for the waiter or waitress.*

In a restaurant:

1. _____

2. _____

3. _____

At the movies:

4. _____

5. _____

6. _____

In your classroom:

7. _____

8. _____

9. _____

1 Read the catalogue page. Then number the pictures to match the descriptions.

□　□　□　□　□

World Tour The Catalogue for Travelers

Every year, World Tour chooses the top five items every traveler must have. Read about what you should buy this year.

1. Digi-2300 Camera $129.99

Every traveler ought to have a good, reliable digital camera. We recommend the Digi-2300. It's small, so you can easily take it anywhere. It's great for taking pictures of landmarks or just for taking pictures of your friends. It's a reasonable price, and it takes great pictures.

2. XP Binoculars $52.99

Look through these fantastic binoculars to see wildlife on your next safari. Using them is a great way to see animals safely and up close. They make the animals look ten times larger. You can also use these binoculars underwater, so they're great for looking at fish, too. They will fit easily in your bag because they're very small. Put them in your bag next to your new camera!

To order, call (800) 555-3400 or visit our website at www.worldtour.com/cup

3. Simple Sarong $18.50

Sarongs are very useful, and there's one size for everyone. Women can use sarongs as a skirt or a dress, but men can use them, too. They work well as towels for the beach or to use after swimming, waterskiing, and kite surfing. Dry your body off, and then the towel dries in minutes! Get it in blue, black, red, orange, or green.

4. Earplugs   2 for $3.50

Earplugs are a cheap and practical gift for a friend or for yourself. Traveling on airplanes, buses, and trains can be noisy, but you won't hear any noise with these earplugs. Put them in your ears and fall asleep!

5. The "It Bag" $75.00

Our best bag is called the "It Bag" because you have to have it! It can be small or large because it's expandable. It's perfect for a day trip or for a weekend vacation. Get it in black, brown, or red.

2 Read the catalogue page again. Then write T (true), F (false), or NI (no information).

1. The binoculars are cheaper than the camera. __T__

2. The camera only comes in one color. _____

3. You have to wear the sarong. _____

4. The earplugs aren't expensive. _____

5. Expanding the bag is easy. _____